THE HABITATION OF DEVILS
Why God Doesn't Act

Revised Edition

Written by Dan R. Overfield

Copyright ©2021 Dan Overfield All rights reserved.

No part of this publication may be reproduced, distributed, or transmitted in any form or by any means, including photocopying, recording, or other electronic or mechanical methods, without the prior written permission of the publisher, except in the case of brief quotations embodied in reviews and certain other non-commercial uses permitted by copyright law.

978-1-8383499-2-9 (Paperback)
978-1-8383499-3-6 (e-book)
978-1-8383938-3-0 (Hard Cover)

Printed in the United States of America

AEGA Design Publishing Ltd
Kemp House, 160 City Road, London
EC1V 2NX United Kingdom
www.aegadesign.co.uk
info@aegadesign.co.uk

The Dedication

This book is dedicated to Christ Jesus our glorious Savior, Redeemer, Creator, King and Friend. This book is also dedicated to His Heavenly Father, Yahweh the Sovereign Lord God Almighty.

May my testimony and witness in the form of this book be pleasing in their sight. I pray their favor to be upon it.

Revelation 4:11 Thou art worthy, O Lord, to receive glory and honor and power: for thou hast created all things, and for Thy pleasure they are and were created.

Revelation 5:13 And every creature which is in heaven, and on the earth, and such as are in the sea, and all that are in them, heard I saying, Blessing, and honour, and glory, and power, be unto Him that sitteth upon the throne, and unto the Lamb for ever and ever.

Amen!

A Tribute to the Love of Children

Oh beautiful children of mine
Who thought their daddy a prince so fine?
Only to discover his shining armor all tarnished
With unknown sins hidden under a coat of faded varnish
Oh beautiful children of mine
From the discovery please take warning
For in this life of sin damaged carnage
Visions of perfect father's fade with the passing of time
Oh beautiful children of mine
Mistakes discovered can become a rich goldmine
If they direct your hearts toward the God of Heaven
Where treasures of grace and forgiveness
Are seventy times seven
Oh beautiful children of mine
My plea for you at this very time
Those revelations of disappointed hopes direct your eyes above
To draw your hearts to the perfect Father of Love
May the Lord of Love in heaven above
Bless you for honoring
This imperfect father with a child's tender and
unconditional love
Oh beautiful children of mine

By Dan R. Overfield

Table of Contents

Chapter 1	*11*
Chapter 2	*14*
Chapter 3	*21*
Chapter 4	*24*
Chapter 5	*33*
Chapter 6	*41*
Chapter 7	*46*
Chapter 8	*54*
Chapter 9	*62*
Chapter 10	*73*
Chapter 11	*82*
Chapter 12	*91*
Chapter 13	*101*
Chapter 14	*112*
Acknowledgement & Review	*145*

The Preface and Purpose

The purpose of this book is fourfold.

First: It is to magnify and bring glory and honor to My Heavenly Father whose name I have come to believe is Yahweh and to His magnificent Son Jesus Christ, for *the great things they have personally done for me.*

Second: It is to reveal the sealing process of God.

While our Heavenly Father is holding back the winds of strife of the seven final deadly plagues, His children (the followers of His Son Jesus Christ) are saved and sealed for all eternity in contrast to those who receive the mark of the beast and are eternally lost. This seal is found in the Ten Commandments that are the expression of His Divine will.

Third: It is an attempt to help those who profess to be followers of Jesus Christ, to make a translation preparation as they travel to the Heavenly Promised land and to the Celestial City.

Fourth: It is to bring hope to the hopeless and an attempt to prevent a needless tragedy happening to those fellow travelers as happened to me.

It has been said that if a person can learn from another's mistake then he/she doesn't have to make the same mistake. My hope and prayer is that by making myself vulnerable, by sharing with you my mistakes, shortcomings and weaknesses then perhaps someone might be saved from the same sort of personal tragedy I experienced. Even if you, the one now reading these words, are the only one, then this effort and labor will not have been in vain.

Yet already you might find yourself caught up in a similar tragic dilemma I found myself in, then perhaps my testimony can *bring hope to you, by revealing God's tender mercy, care and wonderful power that will bring you off more than a conqueror.* If our loving Heavenly Father can take my life, which was a shattered wreck, filled with wretchedness and by His grace, love and power make this life worth living again, full of purpose and meaning, then He can certainly do the same for you.

Additional note: This little book was not written in the style of a biography nor does it read like one. It was not written to entertain but to encourage and edify. It is written as if I were standing before you and sharing with you my experience. My fervent hope is that it will prove to be a blessing to you.

The Introduction

It was a hot summer day in July 1991. I woke up to find myself in an air-conditioned hospital emergency room with an IV needle inserted into my arm. A strange looking device attached to my index finger I was to discover later, after coming out of a deep coma, was a device to measure the oxygen levels in my blood. There was also a blood pressure cuff attached to my other arm and a heart monitor with little green blips moving across the screen. When I tried to move I discovered what I had attached to my body prevented my arms and legs from moving, for they were tied to the bed railings.
Then I started to slowly remember what had happened. The previous night I had attempted to take my own life first by cutting my wrists, and then with a massive overdose of doctor prescribed medications. Here I was a professed Christian, a devoted and loyal convert to the Lord Jesus Christ. Believing that my Lord would protect me from harm and certainly not believing in self- inflicted murder.
How had I come to such a place in my life?

To share the answer to that question, with the desire to help someone else who finds themselves in a dangerous situation greater than themselves, is the reason I am writing this book.
This book has not been written for those who feel or think, spiritually speaking, that they are rich and increased with goods and have need of nothing as they stand before the Lord of glory. It is written for those who like me feel and think they are poor, blind and naked as they stand before the Lord (Revelation 3: 14-18).
There is a saying that goes something like this: "Be careful how you live your life, for your life may be the only Bible some people might read."

What follows is a narrative of my life and the effect the Holy Scriptures have had upon it. I choose to make myself vulnerable for

Christ's sake. In my testimony you will see Christ and His righteousness shining through the obvious cracks and faults of the shattered life of this earthen vessel.

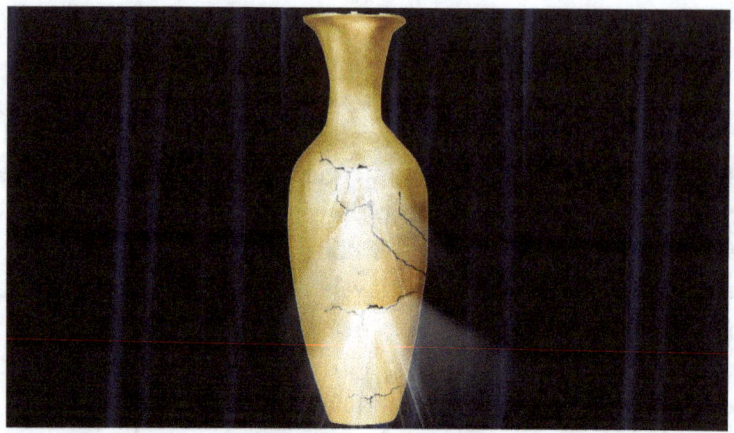

My prayer and hope is that this witness and testimony will be an instrument in His hand to exalt and glorify His name by witnessing to you, what great things the Lord has done for me.

Chapter 1

The Habitation of Devils

REVELATION 18
"1 After these things I saw another angel come down from heaven, having great power: and the earth was lightened with his glory.

2 And he cried mightily with a strong voice, saying, Babylon is fallen, is fallen, and is become **the habitation of devils**, and the hold of every foul spirit, and a cage of every unclean and hateful bird."

As you begin reading this little book, perhaps you find yourself in a similar situation as myself. Struggling to understand why there are so much pain and suffering going on all around you. Do I need to say more about 9/11 or the global war on terrorism? Even while I'm composing my ideas and formatting for this manuscript, a disaster of biblical proportions has hit the Asian coastline. Over 150,000 people are killed and thousands missing and they are still counting. This disaster was caused by the largest

Tsunami in recorded history. Now the United States has experienced another personal disaster with hurricane Katrina destroying most of the Gulf Coast and the destruction of the city of New Orleans, Louisiana. Presently we have rioting, looting, violence and even killings on a alarming scale on our police and citizens.

Perhaps you find yourself caught up in a vortex of your personal pain, trouble, agony, and suffering. Or perhaps you find yourself even in despair of life itself when all you really want is to be happy and to enjoy the simple pleasures of life.

Perhaps you've tried finding relief for your troubled mind, heartache, and suffering by consulting with other people. After all, someone should have the answer to this good and evil business, right?

Perhaps you've considered or had professional therapy, or participated in a support group for troubled and suffering victims of domestic violence, drug abuse, alcohol abuse, criminal behavior, mental or psychological disorders, behavior problems, broken relationships, and divorce.

Perhaps you've experienced the shame, embarrassment, and even ridicule of people who belittle you for being such a poor witness to your so-called Christian faith. Perhaps, just perhaps......

Perhaps you can't understand a God who claims to be your Heavenly Father who would allow all this misery to come upon His children. After all, what kind of human father would not protect his children from harm, heartache, and danger? Perhaps, just perhaps....

After all these efforts on your part to escape the pain, things may seem to be better for a while. Then in the process of time, you find yourself back in the same unending cycle once again, with a broken heart full of pain and heartache wondering why?... why?

I want to share with you what I have discovered in trying to obtain relief from pain and suffering, and understanding about those very things I have mentioned to you in the introduction to this book.

I want to share with you my personal testimony of my deliverance from a very dangerous spiritual deception, that led me to many of those personal afflictions mentioned, that caused so much mental suffering and heartache.

I also want to share with you my personal revelation that took me over twenty-three long, painful, agonizing years to learn and realize.

I hope that this revelation can become a ray of hope, and light upon the pathway of your darkness as you travel the remainder of your life's road. If so, then making myself vulnerable will have been worthwhile. That personal revelation that came to me at a high cost is this:

> That my heart deluded by the world's deception
> and ravished by my careless and reckless attitude
> toward spiritual things had become a place for
> ***"THE HABITATION OF DEVILS"***

DO NOT BE DECEIVED!

Chapter 2

My Journey Begins

During the middle 1600s, John Bunyan penned a book from his prison cell for twelve years. This literary work "The Pilgrim's Progress" has proved over these many years to be a spiritual blessing and help to all that will take the time to read it.

Now it is the middle 2000s and I have penned a book from my spiritual prison cell where I was held captive for twenty-three long years.

I hope that this small literary work will, like John Bunyan's, prove to be a spiritual blessing and help to all that will take the time to read it.

I began my journey through the wilderness of this world walking through the fields of night in spiritual darkness.

Along the way, I would discover what Christian called "his book", only I would call my discovery "my new Book". It would point me in the direction of my newfound destination, the King reigning in the Celestial City in The Heavenly Canaan Land.

Oh, excuse me, I'm getting ahead of my story.

It all began when I was a young boy. My adoptive mother was a professing Christian woman and my adoptive father who was a non-believer that owned and operated his own business that he had named the Arcade Pool Hall and Tavern. Its location was in the rural town of Poplar Bluff, Missouri.

On occasion my mother took me, my brother and sisters to Sunday school and church. If we behaved ourselves (which wasn't too often) she would take us to the youth program called Training Union on Sunday evenings.

Of course, there was also summer Vacation Bible School, and as many of you might recall from your own childhood experience, that was a big fun. Because that was Kool-Aid and cookie time!

As I mentioned earlier in my introduction "Be careful how you live your life for you might be the only Bible some people might ever read." What follows became my Bible of life.

Between Sunday School and my tenure at a local Catholic Grade School, I learned all about the fall of angels and man because of disobedience and sin against the will of their Heavenly Father.

As a child I also loved to hear the story of the beautiful garden, Adam and Eve and that fallen angel Lucifer, who became known as Satan; that evil dragon and serpent that started this whole mess, of the stuff called sin, rebellion, and defiance. (Genesis chapters 1, 2 and 3, Revelation chapter 12: 7-9)

I also used to love to hear the stories about Jesus, His birth in the little stable, and the shepherds and kings that were guided by that bright shining star.

LUKE 2:8-12 And there were in the same country shepherds abiding in the field, keeping watch over their flock by night.
9 And, lo, the angel of the Lord came upon them, and the glory of the Lord shone round about them: and they were sore afraid.
10 And the angel said unto them, Fear not: for, behold, I bring you good tidings of great joy, which shall be to all people.
11 For unto you is born this day in the city of David a Saviour, which is Christ the Lord.
12 And this shall be a sign unto you; Ye shall find the babe wrapped in swaddling clothes, lying in a manger.

I can still hear echoing in the halls of my childhood memory as all of us children softly sang:

> *"Away in the manger a crib for His head*
> *The little Lord Jesus laid down His sweet head*
> *The stars in the sky looked down where He lay*
> *The little Lord Jesus asleep on the hay"*

Can you still hear the little children singing that song?

In Sunday School and Training Union I also learned of Christ's life and how He cared for others:

ACTS 10:38 How God anointed Jesus of Nazareth with the Holy Ghost and with power: who went doing good and healing all that were oppressed of the devil; for God was with Him.

I also learned of Christ's tragic death:

MATTHEW 27:45-50
45 Now from the sixth hour there was darkness over all the land unto the ninth hour.
46 And about the ninth hour Jesus cried with a loud voice, saying, Eli, Eli, lama sabachthani? that is to say, My God, my God, why hast thou forsaken me?
47 Some of them that stood there, when they heard that, said, This man calleth for Elias.
48 And straightway one of them ran, and took a spunge, and filled it with vinegar, and put it on a reed, and gave him to drink.
49 The rest said, Let be, let us see whether Elias will come to save him.
50 Jesus, when he had cried again with a loud voice, yielded up the ghost.

I can still recall singing about the great love that Christ showed by His sacrifice.

Alas! And did my Saviour bleed,
And did my Sovereign die?
Would He devote that sacred head,
For a sinner such as I?

At the cross, at the cross, where I first saw the light,
And the burden of my heart rolled away,
It was thereby faith I received my sight,
And now I am happy all the day.

I also learned about Christ's triumphant and glorious resurrection: **(John 19:41,42 chapter 20:1-20)**

Up from the grave He arose,
With a mighty triumph o'er His foes;
He a-rose a victor from the dark domain,
And He lives forever with His saints to reign.
He a-rose! He a-rose! Hallelujah! Christ a-rose!

Praise the Lord for that glad day!

I also listened to the story of His glorious Second Coming to this old sin-cursed world of ours to take us home to be in a wonderful place called heaven. (I Thessalonians 4:16-17)

Now of course I didn't hear all these Bible stories about Christ in one setting. I learned them each time I attended Sunday School and church. So it went in my childhood days.

Yet as in life, so it was to be in vacation bible school and church, happy moments don't go on forever. For after all the fun time of Kool-Aid and cookies and stories of Jesus meek and mild, came the time to go upstairs into the auditorium and to sit very quietly and listen to the preacher tell of a different kind of Bible story.

Like the frightening story of a thing called the Judgement. A story about a rich man and a poor beggar named Lazarus. A story filled with vivid and graphic scary things like hot flicking flames of hellfire and torment. People writhing in eternal unrelenting and excruciating pain that goes on forever. And forever is for a long long time. (Luke 16:19-31)

The preacher sure knew how to draw out the graphic details of such a horrible and terrible place. He was able to scare the pants off a young boy like me.

At Catholic school, I would also learn a similar place called Purgatory. If you were only sent to this place of burning torment, you could at least have someone help you get out by praying for you or giving money to the church. I apologize for not providing Biblical proof for this story because there is none!

However, as many young boys do, I didn't take the lessons of these thrilling stories to heart. So growing up and discovering myself as a young teen, I found myself less interested in biblical stories and found my love and interest in Christ very superficial. So I gladly accepted a new opportunity that my father presented to me. I wouldn't have to go to church anymore on Sundays. I could earn some money and help him clean up and prepare his pool hall and tavern for the coming business week.

It was quite an offer for a young teen. Now I could save up some money toward buying my wheels! Finally I would be able to buy my own car. Wow! The decision wasn't hard to make. *Next Sunday, I would gladly trade a church pew for a broom and a mop.*

As some of you might have learned by now, whenever you turn away from the things of the Lord, you are headed down a road of big trouble. Of course, I didn't know that then. Hindsight 20-20 you know how that goes.

However, as time continued on, I began fighting against the authority of my parents who in their kindness and concern had adopted all four of us children. The rebellion, quarreling, and fighting at home became so bad and intense that my father, who had a reputation for being confident and able to knock heads together and always win, physically threw me out of the house.

So as a young teenager, I now found myself suddenly faced with the responsibility of caring and providing for myself. I immediately obtained a job, and after some time, asked my high school sweetheart to marry me. Eventually, a short time later I joined the military service and found myself in the middle of a war in a faraway place called Viet Nam.

Now the first phase of my revelation of spiritual ignorance was to begin to reveal itself as the first dark ominous clouds of that ignorance began to thicken and gather around me. They would in time unleash their full and merciless fury upon me.

Chapter 3

Up the Hill of Difficulty, I Go

Along the pilgrim pathway, Christian met two travelers known as "Formalist and Hypocrisy". They traveled together until they came to the foot of a hill, Difficulty. At the bottom of the hill was a spring. There were also two other ways to go, one turned to the left hand and the other turned to the right. But the narrow way went right up the hill called Difficulty.

My teenage and early manhood difficulties began to catch up with me on a hot and sunny day in mid-summer 1970. Three summers before, in 1967, I had returned from my service in Viet Nam. Like many Viet Nam vets, I had to deal with issues from that war but at the age of twenty-three, hey, there wasn't anything I couldn't handle. The sizzling summer day three years later after I returned home, I had just finished a small building project when I noticed an agitation I couldn't shake. I couldn't understand it for there was nothing for me to be agitated about.

That night as the evening drew on, my agitation worsened and suddenly something began to happen to my body that frightened me. It began to convulse violently. I would double over and then my body, with a quick and painful jerk, would arch backward. This went on for hours and hours and was draining my strength. No matter how hard I tried to exercise my will power against its unrelenting force, it was to no avail.

Finally, I was taken to the emergency room of the local hospital where for the first time in my life I was given mind-altering medication to stop the convulsions that enabled me to rest. After a stay in the hospital, I was diagnosed with a condition the physician labeled "war neurosis". Today, it is called Post-Traumatic Stress Disorder or what is known today as PTSD.

A few summers later with chronic and unrelenting headaches (caused by, I believe exposure to agent orange in the war) and frequent medication overdoses to find relief, from recurring nightmares, uncontrollable anger, violent outbursts, and sleepless nights, I found myself locked up in a mental ward. Now to my horror and stunned amazement, I found myself in a new and strange environment. I was staring out a window covered by cold steel bars on the second story of a mental institution.

What a shock that was to my sensibilities. I was to be eventually housed with people walking around like living dead men with sunken and hollow faces. Some with spittle running down the corners of their mouths. Some with their tongues hanging out and just making grunting sounds trying in vain to communicate. Some walking down the halls, zombie-like, having just returned from shock therapy. I kept thinking, *this must be a terrible nightmare, and any moment now, I will be awaken.*

As I stood there in dumb and mind-numbing amazement staring at the people walking in perfect freedom along the sidewalks below me, enjoying the warmth and beauty of a bright sunny day, my mind was carried back to my carefree childhood days; the days when as a young boy with my mother, brother and sisters, we would visit my uncle in the mental ward of the Veterans Administration hospital.

He too was a veteran of a foreign war. He was one of the bravest men who stormed the beaches of Normandy. Now he too was in a vegetative state, with sunken hollow face and eyes. Shell shock was the medical diagnosis then, mockers called him a lunatic and crazy—oh well, you know all the names. But no matter what they label it, or someone mockingly calls it, the result and pain are the same.

As I stood there staring through those ever-confining bars I kept remembering those summer visits to the hospital as a young boy. I could remember saying over to myself, *"I'm not going to be like my uncle, I'm not ever going to be like him."*

Now I found myself painfully asking how did I end up here just like my uncle? *How did I end up just like him?* Mentally ill, crazy, and a lunatic. What am I doing here? What brought me here? How do I get out of here? And how do I get my sanity and my health back? **My God, help me! My God, help me!**

The darkening clouds of my nightmarish dilemma were now beginning to engulf me. Here I was, locked up in a mental institution, recalling as a young boy, a place I vowed never to be. The same as a man, I swore never to be in the same situation. I was crying out to God for help, a God that I did not even know. A God of whom I hadn't ever made the effort to know or even took the time to know. A God I had traded a mop, a broom, and a pool hall for many years ago.

It is written in the Scriptures that, "to everything, there is a season and a time to every purpose under heaven". The time had come for me to get to know the God I had cried to for help.

The doctors had told me that there was no medical cure for my condition. After seeing my dear uncle suffering from his disability, being not much more than a helpless invalid all his remaining life, I knew if I was to regain my mental health again, only the God of Heaven could restore it to me. Thanks to Sunday school and church while a boy growing up, I at least understood that much about God.

Three years had passed since I had experienced my "mental break down" my first experience with "war neurosis" my "PTSD" as they call it. My condition was worsening. I was in and out of hospitals, in and out of mental institutions and clinics, physician after physician, over-doses on medications, sickened with flu-like symptoms twenty-four hours a day, losing job after job. I needed to do something different. Going to another physician or being admitted into another hospital wasn't the answer to the dilemma I found myself in.

Up the hill of difficulty I must go.

Chapter 4

He Touched Me

It had now been three years since my nightmare had began begun on that eventful summer day in 1970. Now on a cold wintry day, in a place called Hot Springs, Arkansas I decided to send for a version of the New Testament I had seen offered on a television program. Now for the first time in my life, I began reading the Scriptures for myself. This time I didn't want to just hear about Jesus meek and mild. *I wanted to understand and experience how He was going to get me out of this terrible dilemma I found myself in*

What happened was a result of that determined effort to discover the God of power, love, and deliverance "happened on this wise" as Christian, of *Pilgrim's Progress* would say.

It was now 1973 and I had recently started working another new job. My little family and I had moved to Hot Springs, Arkansas. After I received my New Testament in the mail, I at once began my search by reading during any spare moment I could take advantage of. Since it was a full-time job, I would rise up early in the morning before anyone else in my family and began to devour my new Book. At work during my lunch hour, I would also go out into my old 1965 Ford pickup truck (Betsy), start the engine, turn on the heater, and continue reading.

As I read day after day, a statement Christ repeated several times in His teachings captivated me. He said, *"whatsoever you shall ask if you believe you shall receive it; you shall have it."*(Mark 11:22-23)

Now that was certainly getting my attention since I had begun to ask and to seek for my mental health restoration. Holding down a full-time job was getting increasingly ever more difficult and I was determined not to lose this new one. During this time I was still under medical care and still taking various and powerful medications.

My newfound fascination with my new Book kept increasing with time. In fact, when I had finished reading the complete Book I began to read it again. With each reading, morning, noon, and evening, those words of Christ stood out in my mind as if they were engulfed in flames. *"Whatsoever you ask in my name I will do it." "If you say to this mountain, move into the sea, it shall be done."* (Matthew 21:21-22)

Then on one cold December during lunch hour, I went out to my truck. The day was December 7, 1973. An eventful day of which was to become a turning point of my life. I continued reading about the Lord Jesus Christ moving mountains and killing fig trees.

Despite the fact I was having mental problems, I still had sense enough to figure out that if I was to walk up to the massive mountain which stood behind my place of employment, and says to it, "mountain of Hot Springs, Arkansas remove yourself and be cast into the sea." I knew full well that mountain wouldn't budge an inch.

Yet at the same time, I wanted with all my heart to believe what Christ was saying to me in the words of His Book, that He would give me what I asked for, if I believe that He would. I was totally confused and wavering between hope for help from Christ to restore my mental health and utter discouragement at the thought of that help only coming from the kind of faith to move mountains. The kind of faith I knew I didn't or couldn't ever possess.

I became highly frustrated and even angry at the thought of how far beyond me any hope of help realistically existed. I just couldn't believe these words I was reading. So in abject despair, I threw my new Book upon the dashboard of my truck.

Yet I still had some time left on my lunch hour so I picked up my new Book again and opened it at a random place to fill the remaining time. There in front of me was a text that glared out before my eyes,

> "Jesus answered and said unto them,
> Verily I say unto you, If ye have faith,
> and doubt not, ye shall not only do this
> which is done to the fig tree, but also if

> ye shall say unto this mountain, Be thou removed, and be thou cast into the sea; it shall be done. *And all things, whatsoever ye shall ask in prayer, believing, ye shall receive.* **Matthew 21: 21**

Well, I thought that certainly was a strange coincidence, it would have to be that text. So once again, I closed my new Book and opened it up, randomly. Again this is the text my eyes fell upon,

> "And Jesus answering saith unto them, Have faith in God. For verily I say unto you, that whosoever shall say unto this mountain, Be thou removed, and be thou cast into the sea; and shall not doubt in his heart, but shall believe that those things which he saith shall come to pass; he shall have what so ever he saith. Therefore I say unto you, What things so ever ye desire, when ye pray, believe that ye receive them, and ye shall have them. **Mark 11: 22-24**

By this time I was really getting upset and agitated for as I said earlier I felt so inadequate and so far removed from the reality of such statements that my frustration level was very high. Also, I was beginning to wonder what was going on here. Turning at random to one of these texts was one thing but turning to two of them in a row and on different pages seemed more than a coincidence. In utter frustration, I flung my new Book onto the dashboard of my truck.

I was perplexed and bewildered by what was going on. What I did next may sound strange to some. (I understand if you chuckle) I closed my eyes and as a blind man would do I, gingerly felt around for it, picked it up, opened it up, all the while with my eyes still tightly closed.

Then as I opened my eyes there in front of me was a text that seemed to glow as if surrounded by flames of fire

I immediately dropped to my knees on the floorboard of "Betsy" and began to weep and pray. My prayer went something along these lines: "Lord----L-O-R-D---**I still need help!** I desire with all my heart to believe what you are clearly saying to me but I just can't believe that I can speak your word to a mountain and it will just disappear. Please forgive me for that and please help me to believe, for in all honesty I can't, yet I want to with all my heart.

What occurred next no human language is enough to express. I had no sooner finished the last word of my prayer of unbelief when suddenly my whole body felt as if I was being totally consumed by burning liquid fire. I seemed to be transported into another dimension as if some fiery chariot was carrying me to some distant place I had never been before. I heard angels singing, surrounding me with their songs. I was totally unaware of time or space. I can't even find words to convey to you all that I experienced on that memorable day.

Only to say that I was keenly aware I was in a very special place.

I had never in my life had a prayer answered like that. I was lost in total wonder and amazement. While kneeling there on the floorboard of my truck I committed my life to the Lord Jesus Christ. He had touched me!

> Shackled by a heavy burden
> Neath a load of guilt and shame
> Then the hand of Jesus touched me
> And now I am no longer the same

The next event I can only recount vaguely because I was in a state of total shock and mind-numbing amazement. My lunch hour was over and it was time to return to work. I recall asking my fellow employee (which had his workstation beside mine) "did I perform my job this afternoon?" He answered "yes" however all I remember is that I walked into my department, sat down at my workstation, and then everyone started milling around to go home, for the workday was over. Four hours had passed in what seemed to be an instant to me.

I drove myself home that cold December evening. *I remember thinking, now all my problems are over, I won't ever be mentally ill or sick again for I had found the Lord.* Everything will be fine from now on. I had now personally discovered that mystic key that allowed me entrance into a brand new dimension of spiritual life. I was in for the surprise and shock of my life!

In an attempt to make a long tragic story short, let me just say that the next twenty- three years were only more of the same. There was no change to my mental suffering at all. I had to learn the deeper things first that would come to explain those words of the Lord that He so strongly impressed upon my mind.

One of these deeper teachings is this: that it is extremely important to understand the words of God correctly. That the way we learned to understand them in the past might not be correct. Even more, a wrong understanding of His Word can lead us to believe that His Words are way over our heads and cannot be materialized or need to be interpreted in different ways. *Therefore by an incorrect interpretation of His Word, we make void the power God has put in them, and we miss out on their fulfillment or even worse we invite danger.*

This is the near-fatal mistake I made that had placed me in that hospital emergency room I told you about at the beginning of my story. The mistake that almost cost me my life. I would discover that I had to learn the truth of this deeper teaching the hard way.

That teaching is this: *We rob God of the power that He has put in His Word by believing an incorrect or deceptive interpretation of His Word, thereby not only missing out on the fulfillment of His Word but even worse, we invite danger with that deceptive interpretation.*

I was soon to discover that another person much wiser than myself and living in Biblical times had to learn that teaching the hard way too.

He is the subject of the next chapter in our continued journey together to understand the deeper things of God and of life.

My Childhood Home

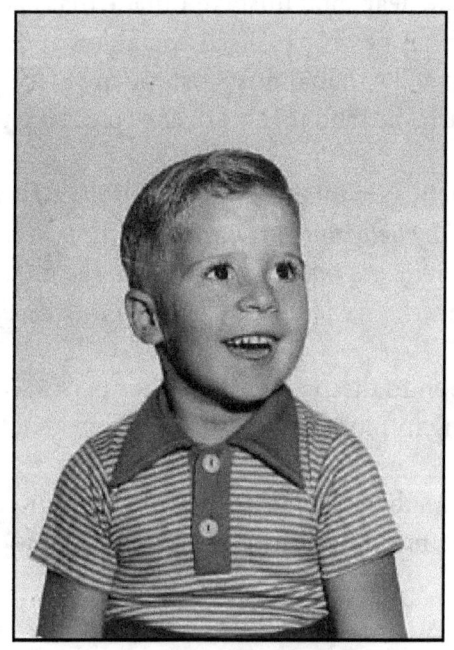

The Young Boy

My Father in his Pool Hall

The Last Remaining Full Photo of "Betsy"

Betsy's "maintenance crew". The legs belong to Dan and his children - Daniel Christopher and Heather Kathleen.

A photo of my father's "Arcade Pool" hall and tavern (the doorway is beneath the large Budweiser sign). My dad is seated on the left side of the famous Budweiser wagon and Clydesdale horses.

Chapter 5

Meeting A Worldly King Along the Way

Now as Christian walked alone in the Way, he spotted someone traveling the same road he was on. He came across the field to meet him and as happenstance would have it; they were crossing the way of each other. The gentleman's name was Worldly Wise man.

As it was with Christian, so it was to be with me. In journeying through my new Book, I too, met a Worldly Wise man. His name was King Nebuchadnezzar. He was the Babylonian king who conquered and destroyed Jerusalem and its magnificent temple in 586BC.

Our paths crossed as the Lord, that was my king now, led me to a special story in my new Book. By now I had just about worn out my New Testament and had purchased a complete Bible (King James Version).

In studying it I read about a king named Nebuchadnezzar *who like me eventually lost his reasoning powers and sanity as a result of believing a dangerous spiritual deception, thereby robbing God of the power and glory due to His Holy Name.* I certainly wasn't on the same status level as a king or great monarch, yet our experiences had some striking similarities. Nevertheless, because of my difficult circumstances, the Lord certainly had my undivided attention by now. The biblical story goes like this:

DANIEL 4

1 Nebuchadnezzar the king, unto all people, nations, and languages, that dwell in all the earth; Peace be multiplied unto you.
2 I thought it good to shew the signs and wonders that the high God hath wrought toward me.

3 How great are his signs! and how mighty are his wonders! his kingdom is an everlasting kingdom, and his dominion is from generation to generation.

4 I Nebuchadnezzar was at rest in mine house, and flourishing in my palace:

5 I saw a dream which made me afraid, and the thoughts upon my bed and the visions of my head troubled me.

6 Therefore made I a decree to bring in all the wise men of Babylon before me, that they might make known unto me the interpretation of the dream.

7 Then came in the magicians, the astrologers, the Chaldeans, and the soothsayers: and I told the dream before them; but they did not make known unto me the interpretation thereof.

8 But at the last Daniel came in before me, whose name was Belteshazzar, according to the name of my god, and in whom is the spirit of the holy gods: and before him I told the dream, saying,

9 O Belteshazzar, master of the magicians, because I know that the spirit of the holy gods is in thee, and no secret troubleth thee, tell me the visions of my dream that I have seen, and the interpretation thereof.

10 Thus were the visions of mine head in my bed; I saw, and behold, a tree in the midst of the earth, and the height thereof was great.

11 The tree grew and was strong, and the height thereof reached unto heaven, and the sight thereof to the end of all the earth:

12 The leaves thereof were fair, and the fruit thereof much, and in it was meat for all: the beasts of the field had shadow under it, and the fowls of the heaven dwelt in the boughs thereof, and all flesh was fed of it.

13 I saw in the visions of my head upon my bed, and, behold, a watcher and a holy one came down from heaven;

14 He cried aloud, and said thus, *Hew down the tree, and cut off his branches, shake off his leaves, and scatter his fruit*: let the beasts get away from under it, and the fowls from his branches:

15 Nevertheless leave the stump of his roots in the earth, even with a band of iron and brass, in the tender grass of the field; and let it be wet with the dew of heaven, and let his portion be with the beasts in the grass of the earth:
16 Let his heart be changed from man's, *and let a beast's heart be given unto him*; and let seven times pass over him.

17 This matter is by the decree of the watchers, and the demand by the word of the holy ones: to the intent *that the living may know that the most High ruleth in the kingdom of men, and giveth it to whomsoever he will*, and setteth up over it the basest of men.

18 This dream I king Nebuchadnezzar have seen. Now thou, O Belteshazzar, declare the interpretation thereof, forasmuch as all the wise men of my kingdom are not able to make known unto me the interpretation: but thou art able; for the spirit of the holy gods is in thee.

19 Then Daniel, whose name was Belteshazzar, was astonied (dazed) for one hour, and his thoughts troubled him. The king spake, and said, Belteshazzar, let not the dream, or the interpretation thereof, trouble thee. Belteshazzar answered and said, My lord, the dream be to them that hate thee, and the interpretation thereof to thine enemies.
20 The tree that thou sawest, which grew, and was strong, whose height reached unto the heaven, and the sight thereof to all the earth;
21 Whose leaves were fair, and the fruit thereof much, and in it was meat for all; under which the beasts of the field dwelt, and upon whose branches the fowls of the heaven had their habitation:
22 It is thou, O king, that art grown and become strong: for thy greatness is grown, and reacheth unto heaven, and thy dominion to the end of the earth.

23 And whereas the king saw a watcher and a holy one coming down from heaven, and saying, Hew the tree down, and destroy it; yet leave the stump of the roots thereof in the earth, even with a band of iron and brass, in the tender grass of the field; and let it be wet with the dew of heaven, and let his portion be with the beasts of the field, *till seven times pass over him*;

24 This is the interpretation, O king, and this is the decree of the Most High, which is come upon my lord the king:
25 That they shall drive thee from men, and thy dwelling shall be with the beasts of the field, and they shall make thee to eat grass as oxen, and they shall wet thee with the dew of heaven, and *seven times shall pass over thee*, till thou know that the most High ruleth in the kingdom of men, and giveth it to whomsoever he will.

26 And whereas they commanded to leave the stump of the tree roots; thy kingdom shall be sure unto thee, after that thou shalt have known that the heavens do rule.
27 Wherefore, O king, let my counsel be acceptable unto thee, and break off thy sins by righteousness, and thine iniquities by showing mercy to the poor; if it may be a lengthening of thy tranquillity.

28 All this came upon the king Nebuchadnezzar.
29 At the end of twelve months he walked into the palace of the kingdom of Babylon.

30 The king spake, and said, Is not this great Babylon, that I have built for the house of the kingdom by the might of my power, and for the honour of my majesty?
31 While the word was in the king's mouth, there fell a voice from heaven, saying, O king Nebuchadnezzar, to thee it is spoken; *The kingdom is departed from thee.*

32 And they shall drive thee from men, and thy dwelling shall be with the beasts of the field: they shall make thee to eat grass as oxen, and *seven times shall pass over thee, until thou know that the most High ruleth in the kingdom of men, and giveth it to whomsoever he will.*

33 The same hour was the thing fulfilled upon Nebuchadnezzar: and he was driven from men, and did eat grass as oxen, and his body was wet with the dew of heaven, till his hairs were grown like eagles' feathers, and his nails like birds' claws.
34 And at the end of the days I Nebuchadnezzar lifted up mine eyes unto heaven, and mine understanding returned unto me, and I blessed the most High, and I praised and honoured him that liveth for ever, whose dominion is an everlasting dominion, and his kingdom is from generation to generation:
35 And all the inhabitants of the earth are reputed as nothing: and he doeth according to his will in the army of heaven, and among the inhabitants of the earth: and none can stay his hand, or say unto him, What doest thou?
36 At the same time my reason returned unto me; and for the glory of my kingdom, mine honour and brightness returned unto me; and my counselors and my lords sought unto me; and I was established in my kingdom, and excellent majesty was added unto me.

37 Now I Nebuchadnezzar praise and extol and honour the King of heaven, all whose works are truth, and his ways judgment: and those that walk in pride he is able to abase.

So there you have it. A story of a king *whose reasoning powers were taken from him by an angel sent from the God of heaven.* The Lord sent His angel to teach this stubborn king a painful yet necessary lesson. That lesson being: *it is dangerous to believe a spiritual deception that robs God of the glory and power of His Word.*

What follows is an insight that the Lord gave to me about the similarities between the king and my experiences regarding this deception.

I have no formal training in a seminary or as a theologian, however, from my bible study and personal spiritual experience, I want to share with you what I think about *the spiritual deception* that the king believed.

Recall the spiritual revelation given to Daniel who gives it to the king in verse 25.

……. seven times shall pass over thee, till thou know that the most High ruleth in the kingdom of men, and giveth it to whomsoever *He will*. (Emphasis on the He, *the Sovereign God of kings GIVES it*). So there was the revelation in the story, yet the king didn't get it!

In verses 29 and 30 he walked around admiring what must have been a splendid view of his famous hanging gardens; those beautiful gardens that were one of the Seven Wonders of the World. Then he said "Is not this great Babylon, that I have built for the house of the kingdom by the might of my power, and for the honour of my majesty?

As the paraphrased version of the Bible puts it: look how great Babylon is! *I built it as my capital to display my power and my might, my glory, and my majesty.*

Now it becomes apparent that the king did not take God at His word and to him, it was of no importance what he believed about the divine revelation given to him. Instead of believing that his kingdom was a *gift from God*, he thought that it was a result of *his own power*, might, and personal effort. *Do you see where the king deceived himself?* King Nebuchadnezzar was about to begin to pay a heavy price for believing that spiritual deception.

> **Daniel 4:31-33** While the word was in the king's mouth, there fell a voice from heaven, saying, O king Nebuchadnezzar, to thee it is spoken; The kingdom is departed from thee.
> **32** And they shall drive thee from men, and thy dwelling shall be with the beasts of the field: they shall make thee to eat grass as oxen, and seven times shall pass over thee, until thou know that the most High ruleth in the kingdom of men, and giveth it to whomsoever he will.

33 The same hour was the thing fulfilled upon Nebuchadnezzar: and he was driven from men, and did eat grass as oxen, and his body was wet with the dew of heaven, till his hairs were grown like eagles' feathers, and his nails like birds' claws.

Instead of the king believing that his kingdom was a gift from God, He thought it was a result of his own power, might, and personal power.

The king had lost it all, his kingship, his kingdom, his dignity, and his sanity. Now for seven long nightmarish and torturous years, he would live no better than an animal. However, the story doesn't end there. As Paul Harvey would say, (I'm showing my age, smile) "stay tuned for the rest of the story."

After seven years of being insane and living more like an animal than a human being, the Lord of Lords and King of Kings honored His Word and gave King Nebuchadnezzar back his reasoning powers, his sanity, his kingdom, and kingship as well.

Daniel 4 :34 And at the end of the days I Nebuchadnezzar lifted up mine eyes unto heaven, and mine understanding returned unto me, and I blessed the most High, *and I praised and honoured him that liveth for ever,* whose dominion is an everlasting dominion, and his kingdom is from generation to generation:
35 And all the inhabitants of the earth are reputed as nothing: and he doeth according to his will in the army of heaven, and among the inhabitants of the earth: and none can stay his hand, or say unto him, What doest thou?
36 *At the same time my reason returned unto me*; and for the glory of my kingdom, mine honour and brightness returned unto me; and my counselors and my lords sought unto me; and I was established in my kingdom, and excellent majesty was added unto me.

So King Nebuchadnezzar, the Worldly Wise man, had learned the hard way to renounce *his spiritual deception, that it doesn't matter if we rob God of His power and glory.* Then he reveled in the joy of embracing the reality of that glorious revelation given to him by that same loving God of all power and all glory.

37 Now I Nebuchadnezzar praise and extol and honour the King of heaven, all whose works are truth, and his ways judgment: and *those that walk in pride he is able to abase.*

I have shared with you the testimony of king Nebuchadnezzar's experience and the glorious light of this revelation dawning upon his darkened mind. Now I want to share with you the similarities of his experience and mine, bringing just like the king, glory and honor to the God of Heaven.

Chapter 6

Walking With A Worldly King

As in the story of the pilgrim, Christian, walking with his friend Hopeful, I too walked with my newfound friend, in my new Book. After being introduced to King Nebuchadnezzar, he and I walked together in our shared experiences. I was to discover in our time together that we both shared similarities in our individual experiences.

The king's belief, that the glory and majesty of his kingdom, were a result of his own efforts and wisdom instead of a gift from the God of Heaven, was his self-deception and direct denial of the revelation given to him by God. Seven long desolate and shameful filled years of insanity and the loss of his reasoning powers were the high prices he paid for his foolishness. He learned it the hard way; *how dangerous it is to believe a spiritual deception.*

In case you're wondering about what is the connection between a pool hall & tavern, a false deceptive teaching, a foolish young man, and a king, I will proceed to connect the dots for you.

Even though on a much smaller social scale, as it was for King Nebuchadnezzar so it was to be with me. I too had to learn the hard way h*ow dangerous it is to believe a spiritual deception.*

As I shared with you in my life story in chapter two I chose to live in the darkness of a dangerous spiritual deception similar to that of the king.

1. We both were introduced to the truth of the Word of God.
2. We both chose to ignore the revelation given to us.
3. The king believed that his life and accomplishments were a direct result of his personal efforts and power.

In other words, he could live his life without God.

4. I too, like the king believed that I could live my life apart from the power of God.

5. The king lived life his way.
6. I lived life my way.
7. We both turned our back on the goodness of the Lord and robbed Him of His majestic glory and power.
8. We both learned the hard way, by our foolish choices, *how dangerous it is to believe a spiritual deception.*

Those are some of the similarities between the king's experience and my own, those are some of the dots connected between a foolish young man and a king, however, there are more, however, I have to return to my life story to show other connections and similarities.

After I had returned home from Viet Nam in 1967, I was still a young man in the flower of my youth and for a youngster or anyone else war is a terrible and destructive experience that will cause you to grow old real fast. I experienced war's destructive power and force in a very personal way. I lost much in Viet Nam, my mental health, my reasoning powers, my self-control, my marital fidelity, my ability to handle stress, even the ability to care for my personal needs and hygiene.

God says, the wages of sin are high and He means what He says. "The wages of sin is death." (Romans 6:23)

How terrible a thing it is, not to be born again, and to know about God yet not know God.

After that first trip to the hospital in 1970, I was now beginning to realize how much I had lost and what serious trouble I now found myself. I was now dealing with a terrible and disabling condition inflicted upon me which Psychiatrists had now diagnosed as PTSD - post-traumatic stress disorder.

During the next two decades, I was admitted, discharged, and readmitted again to many medical and mental institutions. With no less than ten different hospitals including the famous Mayo Clinic and many different physicians all with the same diagnoses—no known cure for PTSD. With symptoms of those suffering from depressive disorders, the unrelenting and never-ending pain of headaches, sickening flu-like symptoms, clinical depression, horror-filled nightmares making sleepless nights seem like an eternity—all draining the life forces out of me.

In addition to my incurable illness, I had to deal with the consequences of earlier foolish choices of my upbringing in my dad's tavern and pool hall. Tobacco addiction from smoking three packs of cigarettes a day, drunken stupors from alcohol abuse, and now I found myself trying more prescription medications. I had been willing to try anything and everything I could that would bring relief to my tormented mind that was now in a state of darkness I had never known before. Despite these medications, I praise the Lord for God-fearing doctors that cared enough to try and help me. It took twenty-three long tumultuous and pain-filled years after returning home from Viet Nam to finally descend into the dark abyss of suicide. On July 5, 1991, I did the unthinkable, I tried to take my own life.

(In an upcoming chapter called "Experiencing the Power of Sin" I spell out in great detail and lessons learned in this awful experience of suicide. For now, I will continue with my life story.)

I had tasted the bitter gall of life, lost, ruined, and devastated from trying to live with an unenlightened mind. It was an attempt to live my life without knowing and understanding the power of God's Word. Living in a delusion as if life consisted of only a giant carnival. The Lord had to send His angel again on the same mission as He did for the king. It's a mission to teach this stubborn and foolish man the painful but necessary lesson of king Nebuchadnezzar. The lesson of a monarch whose reasoning powers were also taken from him by an angel sent from the God of heaven. The same but painful necessary lesson, *that it is dangerous to believe a spiritual deception. That it does matter what we believe.*

- Neither the king nor I behaved like a man created in the image of God.
- The king lost his sanity and became unreasonable for seven years or seven times passing over him.
- My sanity and reasoning powers were adversely affected, sometimes with disastrous results for twenty-three years passing over me.

Yet against this backdrop of hopelessness, darkness, and despair, a bright ray of hope pierces through the dense blackness and gloom. That glorious beam of light was the truth as it is in the person of Jesus Christ.

In my new Book, I seem to hear Christ's voice, saying to me as I read a passage in the book of Isaiah.

Isaiah 46: 9,10 Remember the former things of old: *for I am God*, and there is none else; I am God, and there is none like me,
10 Declaring the end from the beginning and from ancient times the things that are not yet done, saying, My counsel shall stand, and I will do all my pleasure.

My compassionate and loving Savior had seen all along, not only the beginning of my terrifying odyssey but was also telling me *my tormenting ordeal would have an end*. This gave me great hope and an anticipated expectation of deliverance.

However, in my new Book, there was also another lesson to be learned as I waited for the Lord to bring me to the place of deliverance. Theologians call it *discipleship*. I will address this subject in the next chapter along with my experience regarding suicide.

For now, Christ saw the void of understanding that would result from my turning away from the teachings of my early church training.

He saw the seeds of a sin-filled life of filthy language, alcohol, nicotine drug addiction, violence, gambling, prostitution, marital infidelity, and pornography sown in my early childhood while working in my father's pool hall and tavern.

He saw vices of every evil imagination that would be found there and all sown in the mind of a youngster being raised and working in his father's pool hall and tavern. He also saw the horror-filled torture chamber he was destined to go through as a result of his foolish choices.

By the way, I would like to say here at this point, *my father did the best he knew how to raise and provide for me, and I honor him for that*, and I take full responsibility for the foolish decisions I made as a young man.

Yet Christ continued to see my health continuing to deteriorate until I could no longer function in a normal manner or even care for my personal needs. He saw my feeble and futile attempts to obtain a cure by the vast array of compassionate psychiatrists, psychologists, psychotherapists, and medical physicians.

He saw me struggling while admitting myself to rehabilitation and detox centers, pain management clinics, and the list goes on. He finally saw me coming to the end of all my human strength, and resolve in my desperation by attempting to take my own life.

"Be not deceived; God is not mocked: for whatsoever a man soweth, that shall he also reap." **(Galatians 6: 7)**

He saw even my life and spirit being crushed out of me. He saw it all twenty-three years before it happened.

However He also saw *the victory* He had planned all along to give me, at the end of that long hellish ordeal of walking as a foolish worldly-wise man.

Chapter 7

The Assurance of the Coming Victory

During that nightmarish experience of those twenty-three endless years, I also read in my new Book how I could be saved by faith alone in Jesus Christ and His sacrifice. And how important being obedient to His Father's will is. Discipleship as what I believe they call it.

Romans 3:21 – 24 But now the righteousness of God without the law is manifested, being witnessed by the law and the prophets;
22 Even the righteousness of God which is by the faith of Jesus Christ unto all and upon all them that believe: for there is no difference:
23 For all have sinned, and come short of the glory of God;
24 Being justified freely by his grace through the redemption that is in Christ Jesus:

Acts 16: 31 And they said, Believe on the Lord Jesus Christ, and thou shalt be saved, and thy house.
Matthew 7:21 Not every one that saith unto me, Lord, Lord, shall enter into the kingdom of heaven; but he that doeth the will of my Father which is in heaven.

After I had committed my life to the Lord on that cold December morning on the floorboard of my old '65 Ford pick-em-up-truck, I began to sit at the feet of our Lord (devotional time). I spent my time every day to study His Word with a hunger to learn all that He wanted to teach me. He started me out on the milk of His word; forgiveness for the sins of the foolishness of my youth.

Isaiah 1: 18 Come now, and let us reason together, saith the Lord: though your sins are as scarlet, they shall be as white as snow; though they are red like crimson, they shall be as wool.
I Corinthians 6: 9,10 Know ye not that the unrighteous shall not inherit the kingdom of God? Be not deceived: neither fornicators, nor idolaters, nor adulterers, nor effeminate, nor abusers of themselves with mankind,
10 Nor thieves, nor covetous, nor drunkards, nor revilers, nor extortioners, shall inherit the kingdom of God.
Romans 3:12 They are all gone out of the way, they are together become unprofitable; there is none that doeth good, no not one.

Well I certainly fell into many of those categories, yet He continued to say to me, in my new Book:

I John 1:9 If we confess our sins, he is faithful and just to forgive us our sins, and to cleanse us from all unrighteousness. Jesus Christ led me into discovering the wonderful experience of His cleansing blood that washed away all my, guilt and shame for my sins. And returned to me my childhood innocence.

As in Bunyan's story of Christian, the burden of guilt and shame for all the wrongs I had ever committed in my life fell off my back and rolled into the mouth of the sepulcher. **What a joy!** What a wonderful Saviour is Jesus Christ our Lord!

II Corinthians 5:17 Therefore if any man is in Christ, he is a new creature: old things are passed away; behold, all things have become new.

John 15:3 Now ye are clean through the word which I have spoken unto you.

Christ also gave me a new sense of freedom I had never experienced before.

James 1:25 But whoso looketh into the perfect law of liberty, and continueth therein, he being not a forgetful hearer, but a doer of the word, this man shall be blessed in his deed.
John 8:32,36 And ye shall know the truth, and the truth shall make you free.
36 If the Son, therefore, shall make you free, ye shall be free indeed.

He also led me into the glorious miracle of His life-changing power of the new birth experience. He allowed me to taste the tenderness and power of His eternal love that comes from the abiding sense of His strength and care. Of course, you who have accepted our Lord Jesus Christ, as your personal Lord and Savior know what I'm talking about, don't you? I know I'm not telling you anything new.

Yet just as His Word has declared, He will do for us far above what we ask or think. Not only did the Sovereign Lord of Love and Heaven want me to receive blessings and holy joy from receiving the milk of His Word, that is *deliverance and freedom from the guilt of my sin*. He also wanted me, through the study of His Word, *to receive the joy and happiness of freedom from spiritual bondage that comes from the power of sin*.

What a glorious and liberating truth this is!

By the way, just because the Lord wants to give His victory over the power of sin in our lives, doesn't in any way make us sinless.

I John 1:8 If we say that we have no sin, we deceive ourselves, and the truth is not in us.

If you are reading my personal testimony and have never given your life to Jesus Christ and been born again, I would like to offer you an invitation to do so. There are three simple steps for you to do as simple as ABC but eternally profound.

First: Accept- Choose to accept Jesus Christ as your personal Lord and Savior. Remember Jesus Christ is a person, not a fact.
John 1:12 But as many received Him, He gave them the power to become the sons (and daughters) of God, even to them that believe on His name.
Second: Believe - Exercise your faith that God has given to you as a free gift. Believe that you are a child of God, not because of your behavior or your performance but because God has made it a fact.
Acts 16: 31 Believe on the Lord Jesus Christ, and thou shalt be saved....
Thirdly- Confess:
I John 4:15 Whosoever shall confess that Jesus is the son of God, God dwelleth in him and he in God.
So if you have taken those three simple steps then you are a child of the King of the Universe, whether or not you feel like it. **Welcome to the kingdom!**

So to continue with my testimony, despite all the trouble, suffering, and despair I daily found myself in, I was learning liberating truth, day by day, and hour by hour, reading and studying the Word of God for myself.

As I prayerfully read and studied my new Book I came across glorious and encouraging scriptures like these:

Isaiah 43:1-2 But now thus saith the Lord that created thee, O Jacob, and he that formed thee, O Israel, Fear not: for I have redeemed thee, I have called thee by thy name; thou art mine.

2 When thou passest through the waters, *I will be with thee*; and through the rivers, they shall not overflow thee: when thou walkest through the fire, thou shalt not be burned; neither shall the flame kindle upon thee.

Psalms 91:15 He shall call upon me, and I will answer him: *I will be with him in trouble; I will deliver him*, and honour him.

Psalms 37:4-5 Delight thyself also in the Lord, and *he shall give thee the desires of thine heart.*

5 Commit thy way unto the Lord; trust also in him, and *he shall bring it to pass.*

Psalms 32:7 *Thou art my hiding place; thou shalt preserve me from trouble; thou shalt compass me about with songs of deliverance.*

Deuteronomy 7:9 Know therefore that the Lord thy God, he is God, *the faithful God, which keepeth covenant* and mercy with them that love him and keep his commandments to a thousand generations;

Deuteronomy 8:6 Therefore thou shalt keep the commandments of the Lord thy God, to walk in his ways, and to fear him.

Through all these texts I seemed to hear the Lord say to me through His Holy Spirit:

"Dan, I will go through this thing with you and I will deliver you. I will never leave you or forsake you. Just trust Me and don't let go of your love and commitment to me."

Through His Words of my new Book He seemed to be saying to me:

"I want to teach you how to overcome the enemy of your soul and your happiness. *I will empower you to overcome the one who has inflicted this spiritual darkness and this spiritual and physical suffering upon you.*" I began to wonder, "Was the correct understanding of His Word the key to my healing?"

Next, the Lord led me to the following texts and promises to help me to understand how He was going to help me to obtain that key. By enabling and empowering me with His Holy Spirit to overcome the enemy of the soul.

Isaiah 54:17 No weapon that is formed against thee shall prosper, and every tongue that shall rise against thee in judgment thou shalt condemn. This is the heritage of the servants of the Lord, and their righteousness is of me, saith the Lord.
Deuteronomy 28:13 And the Lord shall make thee the head, and not the tail, and thou shalt be above, and thou shalt not be beneath; if that thou hearkens unto the commandments of the Lord thy God, which I command thee this day, to observe and to do them:
Psalms 56:9 When I cry unto thee, then shall mine enemies turn back: this I know; for *God is for me.*
Deuteronomy 28:10 And the people of the earth shall see that thou are calledby the name of the LORD: and they shall be afraid of thee.
Luke 10:19 Behold, *I give unto you power* to tread on serpents and scorpions, and *over all the power of the enemy*: and nothing shall by any means hurt you.
Revelation 12:11 And t*hey overcame him by the blood of the lamb, and by the word of their testimony,* and they loved not their lives unto the death.

In His word, I heard Him saying to me *"I will teach you how to overcome the great adversary of your joy and happiness - by the blood of the lamb."*

The Lord also said to me through His Word:
Revelation 2:7,11,17,26, He that hath an ear, let him hear what the Spirit saith unto the churches; *To him, that overcometh will* I give to eat of the tree of life, which is in the midst of the paradise of God.
11 He that hath an ear, let him hear what the Spirit saith unto the churches; *He that overcometh* shall not be hurt of the second death.
17 He that hath an ear, let him hear what the Spirit saith unto the churches; *To him that overcometh* will I give to eat of the hidden manna and will give him a white stone and in the stone,

a new name is written, which no man knoweth saving he that receiveth it.

26 And *he that overcometh*, and keepeth my works unto the end, to him will I give power over the nations:

Revelation 3:5,11,12-22 *He that overcometh*, the same shall be clothed in white raiment, and I will not blot out his name out of the book of life, but I will confess his name before my Father, and before his angels.

11 Behold, I come quickly: h*old that fast which thou hast, that no man take thy crown.*

12 *Him that overcometh* will I make a pillar in the temple of my God, and he shall go no more out: and I will write upon him the name of my God, and the name of the city of my God, which is new Jerusalem, which cometh down out of heaven from my God: and I will write upon him my new name.

21 *To him that overcometh will* I grant to sit with me in my throne, even as I also overcame, and am set down with my Father in his throne.

22 He that hath an ear, let him hear what the Spirit saith unto the churches.

So it was clear to me that the Lord had wanted to teach me how to overcome the adversary of my soul. He wanted to give me the victory over my terrible mental and spiritual dilemma I found myself after the war.

But how does that work in a practical sense, I asked myself, *"How does that translate into reality?"* How do I get from the words on pages of my new Book, to the liberation those words were holding out to me?

I needed an answer to these questions.
My mind carried me back to that cold December day in Betsy:

"And Jesus answering saith unto them,
have faith in God. For verily I say unto you,
That whosoever shall say unto this mountain,
Be thou removed, and be thou cast into the
sea; and shall not doubt in his heart, but shall

believe that those things which saith shall come to pass; he shall have what so ever he saith. Therefore I say unto you, What things so ever ye desire, when ye pray, *believe* that ye receive them, and ye shall have them.
Mark 11: 22-24

    I must exercise faith in the power of God's Word and believe what he is saying to me is true. *What God promises He will do; He will do!*

    This was the stream of light that would pierce my darkened understanding of God's Word. This was the holy and sacred joy received from Christ which not only delivered me from all the guilt and shame of my former sins, but *now was to deliver me from the spiritual bondage which came as a result of the power of those sins.* Glory and honor to His Holy Name! Praise my Savior in holy joy for His wonderful goodness and the blessed assurance of salvation.

> *Blessed assurance Jesus is mine!*
> *Oh, what a foretaste of glory divine!*
> *Heir of salvation, purchase of God,*
> *Born of His Spirit, wash'd in His Blood.*

Chapter 8

Experiencing the Power and Consequences of Sin
(Walking with Christian in the Valley of the Shadow of Death)

As shared in the previous chapter, faith was the key that unlocked the mysteries of God. Yet I needed more than faith, I also needed the wisdom and understanding that God had promised to me in my new Book.

Proverbs 2:1-6 My son, if thou wilt receive my words, and hide my commandments with thee;
2 So that thou incline thine ear unto wisdom, and apply thine heart to understanding;
3 Yea, if thou criest after knowledge, and liftest up thy voice for understanding;
4 If thou seekest her as silver, and searchest for her as for hid treasures;
5 Then shalt thou understand the fear of the Lord, and find the knowledge of God.
6 For the Lord giveth wisdom: out of his mouth cometh knowledge and understanding.
James 1:5 If any of you lack wisdom, let him ask of God, that giveth to all men liberally, and upbraideth not (without reproach); and it shall be given him.

The reason that I needed more wisdom and understanding, was that despite the dedication of my life to the Lord Jesus Christ on the floorboard of "Betsy" on that chilly December morning in 1973, this business of being free from mental problems and spiritual bondage and oppression kept eluding me.

My mental problems worsened with time. I had now come to a place sixteen years later where I could no longer be gainfully employed (that's how the physicians put it). And I could no longer support myself financially.

That surprise and shock came after I had discovered that mystical key that unlocked a new spiritual dimension for me. Yet it never ceased to be just that, a surprising shock for the next twenty-three seemingly endless years. I had in my youth, sown to the wind and I would reap a whirlwind.

Yet while I studied my new Book every day, the Holy Spirit continued to lead me.

I Corinthians 2:10 But God hath revealed them unto us by his Spirit: for the Spirit searcheth all things, yea, the deep things of God.

He led me not only to the Old Testament story of King Nebuchadnezzar, but also to another story I discovered in the New Testament. A story that I was also able to recognize some similarities to my life.

This revelation was more frightening to me than the previous one of the similarities with the Babylonian king.

It was the story of the demoniac found in the gospel of Mark Chapter 5. Like the story of King Nebuchadnezzar, not every aspect of the story pertains to my testimony. However as I did in the story of the King, I want to share the whole biblical narrative with you, then highlight the similarities to my experience.

> **Mark 5: 1-20** And they came over unto the other side of the sea, into the country of the Gadarenes.
> 2 And when he was come out of the ship, immediately there met him out of the tombs *a man with an unclean spirit,*
> 3 Who had his dwelling among the tombs; and no man could bind him, no, not with chains:
> 4 *Because that he had been often bound with fetters and chains,* and the chains had been plucked asunder by him, and the fetters broken in pieces: neither could any man tame him.
> 5 And always, night and day, he was in the mountains, and the tombs, crying, and cutting himself with stones.
> 6 *But when he saw Jesus afar off, he ran and worshipped him,*

7 And cried with a loud voice, and said, What have I to do with thee, Jesus, thou Son of the most high God? I adjure thee by God, that thou torments me not.
8 *For he said unto him, Come out of the man, thou unclean spirit.*
9 And he asked him, What is thy name? And he answered, saying, *My name is Legion: for we are many.*
10 And he besought him much that he would not send them away out of the country.
11 now there was there nigh unto the mountains a great herd of swine feeding.
12 And all the devils besought him, saying, Send us into the swine, that we may enter into them.
13 And forthwith *Jesus gave them leave. And the unclean spirits went out,* and entered into the swine: and the herd ran violently down a steep place into the sea, (they were about two thousand;) and were choked in the sea.
14 And they that fed the swine fled, and told it in the city, and in the country. And they went out to see what it was that was done.
15 and they come to Jesus, and *see him that was possessed with the devil*, and had the legion, sitting, and clothed, and *in his right mind*: and they were afraid.
16 And they that saw it told them how it befell to him that was possessed with the devil, and also concerning the swine.
17 And they began to pray him to depart out of their coasts.
18 And when he had come into the ship, he that had been possessed with the devil prayed him that he might be with him.
19 Howbeit *Jesus* suffered him not, but *saith unto him, Go home to thy friends and tell them how great things the Lord hath done for thee, and hath had compassion on thee.*
20 And *he departed and began to publish* in Decapolis *how great things Jesus had done for him*: and all men did marvel.

Mark 5:2 There met him (Christ) a man (Dan) with an unclean spirit:

As I shared with you at the beginning of my testimony, I met Jesus Christ on the floorboard of my 1965 Ford pick-up truck. That was on December 7th, 1973. I previously had a "mental breakdown" diagnosed as "war neurosis" or "PTSD" in the summer of 1970.

My medical records testify of my progressively disabling condition. The physician's diagnoses of my mental incapability were also at the same time an indicator of my spiritual problems. *In biblical terms, a man who is insane is a man with an unclean spirit.*

When this truth was brought home to me, I was horrified. For many years I refused to accept that I, who had given my life and heart to Jesus Christ and whose sins were forgiven could be possessed with demonic spirits.

The depth of my ignorance of my spiritual deception and condition concerning biblical truth cost me many additional years of spiritual bondage. *When I met Christ I was a man with an unclean spirit.* I was to learn that demonic spirits were creating havoc in my new born again life.

Mark 5:4 Because that he had been often bound with fetters and chains:

I have shared with you how I was confined to mental institutions. Not only behind barred windows and locked doors, but also chemically. It's truly an eye-opening and difficult experience.

Mark 5:5 Cutting himself:

In *Pilgrims Progress*, Christian came to a place called "the valley of the shadow of death" after passing through the "valley of humiliation".

"Now Christian must need to go through it for the way to the Celestial City passes right through it. Here, poor Christian was hard put to it. Here in this valley of the shadow of death, Dan was hard put to it."

On the night of July 5, 1991, I did the unthinkable. I attempted to take my life by *cutting my wrist* with a knife. When that didn't work, I took a massive overdose of prescription medications, which plunged me into a deep coma and almost cost me my life.

If not for the direct intervention from the Lord, an emergency phone call from my former wife, some well-trained professional paramedics and hospital staff, I would not be here today sharing this testimony of the goodness and kindness of the Lord with you. I want to praise Him, my Lord and Savior and thank each of those involved for the role they played in my rescue from the brink of death.

While we are at this place in my testimony, I want to take this opportunity to share with you this business of suicide. Have you ever heard the saying, "things aren't always what they seem"? I discovered the truth of this statement in my suicide experience.

Growing up as a youth, I had often read or seen portrayed in movies about people in desperation and helplessness taking their own lives. I recall one scene where a beautiful young woman on a dark and moonlit night walked glassy-eyed and stone-faced into the incoming waves breaking upon the beach of the ocean and drowned herself.

I often wonder how can a person be in such a state of mind? When feeling the ocean waves splashing upon her and hearing the roaring of those waves, makes the conscious decision to breathe in water instead of air? How could one go through that process and then follow through with that decision?

I wonder, was there a sinister power possessing her and controlling her actions?

After my personal experience with this traumatic tragedy of attempting self-inflicted death, I have gained insight into an experience I wish I hadn't gained. However, since I can't change the past and now have this insight, I would like to share it with you for your benefit. God forbid you would ever need this insight. It went like this:

First of all, it wasn't planned. There was no forethought of how it was to be carried out. I hadn't written any suicide notes to be left behind explaining how or why.

The act itself caught me by surprise. Words can't express the depths of human despair that by then twenty-three years of suffering daily, hourly, weekly, yearly with this terrible affliction had brought me too. I was finally brought to the place where I had no more internal strength to fight against it any longer.

I was trying to draw strength from my well of internal strength with a bucket that was dragging against hard rock bottom. Pulling up nothing but emptiness. I had nothing left to bravely battle against this overwhelming dilemma I found myself in.

Along with my increasing disabling condition, I now had to face the spiritual reality of demonic possession. That realization, with the inability to fight any longer against it, allowed the weight of despair to crush out what remaining desire to live I had left in me. I was helpless against it. What happened next may sound unbelievable but this is how it happened. This is the way I experienced the incident.

I was now bedridden, struggling with the pain and suffering from all those accumulated years, when suddenly the heaviness of the weight of despair rolled over me like a giant asphalt steam-roller squeezing that mystic wonder called life out of my very being. Then I saw and felt the power of life caught up in a giant vortex and being emptied out of me.

The closest illustration I can come up with would be like a small ship whirling around in a vortex of a giant whirlpool out in the middle of the ocean. I was completely helpless to prevent it from happening.

As soon as the power of life left me, an evil spirit appeared in front of me and then took complete possession of me, by excerising his authority over me. *I was to learn later that his name was called Suicide.*

For that moment, I only knew I was completely powerless against him and I subject to his authority and power. *The power of sin and its consequences were about to engulf me.*

The first thing he commanded me to do was to pick up the small knife I had laying there and cut my wrists (I only used it as a letter opener because it was so dull.) If it hadn't been so serious, this next part would seem funny (I understand if you again chuckle).

I began to reason with the creature and I said to him "that knife wouldn't cut a hot butter" - so who was he kidding? He told me in a very commanding voice to do it anyway. I had no power to resist his authority so I began to cut my wrists and as predicted, it was only

cutting my skin superficially not reaching the main arteries.
I remember telling him "see, I tried to tell you" but he retorted "keep cutting" - so I did.

After it became evident, I couldn't really harm myself seriously in this manner the demonic spirit named *Suicide* demanded that I look down onto the floor where my briefcase was lying open. Inside it were vials of medications of all types including tranquilizers, uppers, downers, sleeping and narcotic pain medications I had accumulated over the years.

I looked down at them as he had told me to do, then he commanded me "pick all the bottles of medication one at a time and take all of them". I remember saying to him in astonishment "all of them? That will kill me!" He said "I know."

So I did as he had commanded me. I can't express to you the surreal feeling that I was experiencing at that moment. It just didn't seem real that I had no power to resist his commands. *I was completely subject to his authority.*

I can't share with you how many pills I took, but it was enough to complete the task I was given to do. I began to feel myself slipping into deep darkness. Just before I lost consciousness, by and only by the grace of God I managed to pick up the phone and call long distance to my wife who was not there at that time. I was barely able to tell her what I did. Before I could explain more of what had happened, I slipped into the darkness that was engulfing me.

She called the paramedics and they came and rushed me to the hospital. By the time they got to the house, I was in a deep coma.

Thanks to the Lord's grace, my former wife, and those caring and professional paramedics and emergency room doctors and technicians, I can share this testimony with you in this little book.

My life had been spared and the rest of the story you know, as I shared it with you in the introduction portion of this book. **To Jesus Christ be the glory for the great things He has done!**

As I told my physician's nurse "Christ was with me before this experience. Christ was with me, in and through this experience, and Christ was still with me when I came out of the experience". In fact, I came out of the experience with a brand new confidence in my love and relationship with the Lord.

Romans 8:35-39 Who shall separate us from the love of Christ? shall tribulation, or distress, or persecution, or famine, or nakedness, or peril, or sword?
36 As it is written, For thy sake we are killed all the day long; we are accounted as sheep for the slaughter.
37 Nay, in all these things we are more than conquerors through him that loved us.
38 For I am persuaded, that neither death, nor life, nor angels, nor principalities, nor powers, nor things present, nor things to come,
39 Nor height, nor depth, *nor any other creature, shall be able to separate us from the love of God, which is in Christ Jesus our Lord.*
(Not even if it's the hideous demonic creature of Suicide.)

    The Lord and my relationship with Him stayed intact through the whole ordeal. Because when I came to the end of my resources and hope; that was the place where I found their brightest fulfillment. Praise Him! Praise Him! Praise Him!

> Praise Him! Praise Him! Jesus our blessed Redeemer!
> Sing, O Earth, His wonderful love proclaim!
> Hail Him! Hail Him! highest archangels in glory;
> Strength and honor give to His holy name!

    This is why I stated earlier "things are not always as they appear". It appeared that I planned and committed suicide. Yet it was not attempted suicide it was spiritual murder, *the result of the consequence of believing a spiritual deception that robbed God's Word of its glorious power.*

    You see, believing the truth versus believing a deception is a serious business. I know and I learned it the hard way. But as a saintly and elderly gray-haired lady once told me "experience is a hard teacher but he delivers the goods."

    The Lord had taught me by experience, the power, and the consequences of sin.

Chapter 9

Experiencing the Power and the Consequences of Victory
(Victory over Apollyon)

> **Mark 5:6** But when he saw Jesus afar off,
> he ran and worshipped him:

This next part of my testimony is hard to express and explain. How does a person who is possessed by demonic spirits worship and fellowship with God?

I kept asking the question, *"how could I have the same problems that this demoniac of the gospel of Mark had since I had previously committed my life to the Lord Jesus Christ?"*

I was terrified at the thought of the similarities I saw and experienced in this gospel story.
The Lord then reminded me of another scripture in my new Book.

> **Galatians 6:7** Be not deceived; God is not mocked: for whatsoever a man soweth, that shall he also reap.

I heard the Lord give me an answer to my prayerful and honest question about this scripture and by my experience. He was telling me WHY HE DOESN'T ACT, always in the way we think He will act. In my case, it was because that *"I had given myself into the hands of the enemy while growing up in my father's pool hall and tavern and that I had given the adversary an absolute right to oppress and possess me."* I had sown to the wind and I must reap the whirlwind with that decision so many years

However, I also heard Him say to me…

"Dan, I will go through this thing with you and I will deliver you. I will never leave you nor forsake you. Just trust Me and don't let go of your love and commitment to me."

I would have liked to say that I was like a righteous Job.

The Lord allowed the adversary to attack him to test his fidelity and loyalty to God. But I have to admit the foolishness of my personal decision, and need to own up to the responsibility of that decision. Yet the Lord in His great wisdom and compassion used the foolishness of that decision, to test my love and fidelity to him after I gave my heart to Him so many years later on the floorboard of that old Ford pick up truck.

However, in His great mercy and love, He bore long with me and kept yet another promise made to me in my *new Book*.

I Corinthians 10:13 There hath no temptation taken you but such as is common to man: but God is faithful, who will not suffer you to be tempted above that ye are able; but will with the temptation also make a way to escape, that ye may be able to bear it.

So not only did the Lord deliver me from the torment and torture of my mind, but He also used the adversary's attacks against me for my good and benefit. How did He do that? By using my twenty-three year living nightmare to illuminate my mind, clearing up misconceptions I had about spiritual truth. Filling my mind with His wisdom and understanding in regards to these deep issues of life, pointing out my spiritual deception that His Word had been robbed of its power in my life. His wisdom would teach me to recover that power and cause me to praise His Name, His Wisdom, His Power, and His Might!

Mark 5: 8,9,13
8 For he said unto him, Come out of the man, thou unclean spirit.
9 And he asked him, What is thy name? And he answered, saying my name is Legion: for we are many.
13 Jesus gave them leave. And the unclean spirits went out:

As Christian continued his journey to the Celestial City, he met in his path a fiendish creature named "Apollyon". He was a hideous monster, foul and disdainful. I, too, had an encounter with my own personal "Apollyon".

This next part of my witness will be the "nuts and bolts", so to speak, of how the Lord Jesus Christ through the Holy Spirit delivered me from demonic spirits (my Apollyon alongside with Suicide) that were wreaking havoc and despair in my life. I share it with you, hoping that it may help you with your encounter with your own personal demons.

Despite still being puzzled about this issue of how to translate my new found faith in God's Word, the following gave me hope.

> Believing I would receive,
> that which I believed I would receive,
> if only I would believe, I would receive it.
> Get it!

But I needed to understand this overcoming business by the blood of the lamb. So I took the matter to the Lord in prayer.

In His mercy for my ignorance and His Providence, He sent into my life a retired minister who mentored me on the subject. As a result of following his wise counsel, I came to understand that the power to overcome this demonic spiritual influence in my life was to exercise faith. A *faith in the blood of the Son of God* that was shed for me on Calvary two thousand years ago. In other words, just as I had believed that the blood of Christ cleansed my heart from the guilt of my former sins and future sins, I needed to believe that faith in His blood would cleanse me from the power of sin. That same power to be exercised against the terrible demonic forces working to destroy my happiness and life.

So my prayers now took on a form of a spiritual warfare prayer, something like this. In an audible voice, I would say,

"You evil and demonic spirit, you are the adversary of the Lord Jesus Christ. Christ rebukes you and I exercise His authority over you and I bring His blood against you. You will leave my presence and no longer torment me!" Then I prayed: *"Heavenly Father would you have*

your holy angels bind this evil spirit and remove him from me. I ask this in the name of the Lord Jesus Christ."

I would then exercise my faith by believing that His angels will do as He commands them and the evil spirit would leave me. And as they left, they did it in different ways. As some of the Biblical accounts, some left screaming, some threatening, some making my body convulse or my mouth salivating and foaming. Some yelled out mockingly and cursing at God with great anger pleaded to be left alone.

Mark 5:13 Jesus gave them leave and the unclean spirits went out – **ALL 300 OF THEM!**

So despite the battle I had with the evil spirits and with the spirit of suicide in my personal "valley of humiliation", I continued to hold on to my spiritual sword (the word of God) and my newfound faith.

Ephesians 6:16-17 Above all, taking the shield of faith, wherewith ye shall be able to quench all the fiery darts of the wicked. 17 And take the helmet of salvation, and the sword of the Spirit, which is the word of God.

Each time I prayed this warfare prayer, no sooner would one demonic spirit leave, then another would be manifested and the whole process would begin anew. By prayer and fasting, this process went on non stop for eight exhausting days and eight sleepless nights.

Micah 7:8 Rejoice not against me, O mine enemy: when I fall, I shall arise; when I sit in darkness, the LORD shall be a light unto me.

Romans 8:37 Nay, in all these things we are more than conquerors through him that loved us.

The Lord Jesus Christ under the power of His shed blood, won the day, and a twenty-three-year living nightmare was ended and I was set free from a hoard of demonic spirits who were vanquished that glad day, all three hundred of them. Peace and sense of well being came over me that was heavenly. Praise His glorious name!

Revelation 12:11 And they overcame him by the blood of the lamb, and by the word of their testimony;

***

All hail the power of Jesus name! Let angel's prostrate fall;
Bring forth the royal diadem, And crown Him Lord of all;
Bring forth the royal diadem, and crown Him Lord of all.
Hail Him who saves us by His grace And crown Him Lord of all.

That memorable week and experience ended on June 17, 1993. The Lord kept His promise to me when He had said to me years before *"I will teach you how to overcome the great adversary of your joy and happiness by the blood of the lamb."*

However, despite the glorious victory Christ had given to me, I discovered that this was an ongoing process. The archenemy of our soul and wellbeing won't give up that easily.

Once again, I was surprised for I thought that after the mighty victory the Lord had given me, all their attacks and oppression would end. Uh-uh.

Evil angels (demons) still crowd around me pressing darkness upon me, trying to shut out Jesus from my view. Their goal is to lead me to focus on the continuing trouble and harassment and lead me to distrust God and become bitter toward Him for allowing the enemy to bring such trouble and problems against me.

Jesus tells the story full of wisdom from Heaven. The story goes like this:

Matthew 12: 43-45 When the unclean spirit is gone out of a man, he walketh through dry places, seeking rest, and findeth none.

44 Then he saith, I will return into my house from whence I came out; and when he comes, he findeth it empty, swept, and garnished.
45 Then goeth he, and taketh with himself seven other spirits more wicked than himself, and they enter in and dwell there: and the last state of that man is worse than the first. Even so, shall it be also unto this wicked generation.

    I have discovered my only safety is to keep my mind stayed upon the Lord Jesus Christ by constantly spending devotional time, focusing my mind upon Him and not on the problems, pain, or trouble. Christ's angels have been given charge over us and they are continually wafting their wings over us to scatter and dispel the thick darkness.

    The angels hasten to our assistance as long as we continue to persevere in our struggle to call upon God for help and deliverance.

John 15: 4-5 Abide in me, and I in you. As the branch cannot bear fruit of itself, except it abide in the vine; no more can ye, except ye abide in me.
5 I am the vine, ye are the branches: He that abideth in me, and I in him, the same bringeth forth much fruit: for without me ye can do nothing.

    How much is nothing? That is "0" with the peeling removed! Human effort is helpless when combating demonic forces. Christ alone through the angency of the Holy Spirit must win the day. We must choose by faith to let Him accomplish that we cannot do, and that's not always easy to accomplish. (**Zechariah 4:6**)

Satan's evil angels still press around me, causing me much suffering and distress. But they have no power over me now, for I have obtained the victory freely given to me by the grace and righteousness of our Lord and Savior Jesus Christ. He has clothed me with the armor of God and empowered me to resist the spiritual power of the enemy's evil. The joy of the Lord is now my strength!

Ephesians 6:10-18 Finally, my brethren, be strong in the Lord, and in the power of his might.
11 Put on the whole armour of God, that ye may be able to stand against the wiles of the devil.
12 For we wrestle not against flesh and blood, but against principalities, against powers, against the rulers of the darkness of this world, against spiritual wickedness in high places.
13 Wherefore take unto you the whole armour of God, that ye may be able to withstand in the evil day, and having done all, to stand.
14 Stand therefore, having your loins girt about with truth, and having on the breastplate of righteousness;
15 And your feet shod with the preparation of the gospel of peace;
16 Above all, taking the shield of faith, wherewith ye shall be able to quench all the fiery darts of the wicked.
17 And take the helmet of salvation, and the sword of the Spirit, which is the word of God:
18 Praying always with all prayer and supplication in the Spirit, and watching thereunto with all perseverance and supplication for all saints;

Since that glorious miracle of June 17th, 1993, the Lord has continued to promise me another of His wonderful miracle's that is found in the book of Jeremiah:

Jeremiah 30:17 For I will restore health unto thee, and I will heal thee of thy wounds, saith the Lord.

This miracle has also been a long and ongoing process, going on forty-seven years now. Just as the evil one did to Christ after His victory in the wilderness, harassing, oppressing, and contesting His every advancing step in life, so it was, too be in my experience. To this day, I still have to struggle against and deal with the aftermath of the difficult consequences resulting from my misuse of mind-altering medications. Faith enables me to continue. It doesn't make it easy but it does make it possible.

I Timothy 6:12 Fight the good fight of faith, lay hold on eternal life, whereunto thou art also called, and hast professed a good profession before many witnesses.

For I have done damage to my body and brain with so many overdoses and so many years of narcotic medication.

Yet once again, because of His gracious love and mighty power, instead of lying in a hospital bed, or looking out from between steeled-barred windows, or lying on a death bed, *I am writing this book, and giving the word of my testimony to the glory of His Name.*

Yes, this is a modern-day miracle sent from Heaven's Throne of Love. That a man with a mental breakdown, a man that damaged his brain by abusing drugs, this same man has by the grace and love of Almighty God accomplished a challenging achievement of sharing the word of his testimony with you in the form of this book.

Jesus said to Dan "Go home to thy friends, and tell them *how great things the Lord hath done for thee*, and hath had compassion on thee. So he departed and *began to publish how great things Jesus had done for him.* Mark 5:19,20

Although the writing of this book was seventeen years in the making, I did not become disheartened or discouraged, for after all, it took Noah 120 years to accomplish the impossible.

I publish it now.

At this point you might be asking, why since he had this wonderful conversion experience back in 1973, why does he publicly publish it just now? The answer is this—Christ has said "Behold I make all things new". And by faith, Christ fulfilled this wonderful promise to me the instant I gave my heart and life to Him.

However, it took many years of treatment in and out of treatment centers and hospitals. It also took years to recover from two divorces. It too took many months to recover from a jeep accident that almost cost me my life. It took years to obtain deliverance from being a chain smoker , a drunkard, and a man that settled arguments with violence. It took years to deal with the consequences of my sinful lifestyle. It also took me years to write this book that is now being revised. I could go on and on, but I think you get the idea. Because of my disability and my love for my sinful lifestyle, everything the Lord accomplishes through me has been an uphill battle.

I have heard testimonies of people that got instant deliverance from and over their sins and shortcomings, but that hasn't been my experience. I envy them and am happy for them for their glorious experience. However, that is not how the Lord has dealt with me.

Christ has His way of keeping me completely dependent upon Him, each and every moment of the day.

As He did with the apostle Paul, He has left a messenger of Satan to buffet me, by allowing my on-going symptoms of PTSD with chronic headaches to still plague me to this day. It is my personal "thorn in my flesh".

God in His infinite Wisdom has seen fit to agree with the doctors,(at least for now) that there is no cure for PTSD. It appears that the flaws in this earthen vessel will stay with me for the remaining years of my life in this sin-damaged world.

II Corinthians 4:7 But we have this treasure in earthen vessels, that the excellency of the power may be of God, and not of us.

Like Paul, the Lord has told me to quit asking Him to remove it from me. Yet I still long to be finally rid of it. And like the apostle Paul, we all have our own personal "thorns in the flesh". We all have our personal demons we have to deal with. So how in the world, as sinful and sin damaged people (flawed vessels Romans 3:23 For all have sinned, and come short of the glory of God.) how then are we to stand before a holy God; Jesus Christ at His second coming?

The answer to this dilemma is found in what Christ has taught us in the parable of the vineyard. Remember what He said that I shared with you in the previous chapter.

John15:4 Abide in Me, and I in you. Verse 5 ..for without Me you can do nothing. That's "0" with the peeling removed. Remember?

So by the sovereignty of Christ's marvelous grace, we can stand before a holy God, Jesus Christ, King of creation yet the friend of sinners. PRAISE HIS WONDERFUL NAME!

Colossians 1: 27 To whom God would make known what is the riches of the glory of this mystery among the Gentiles, which is Christ in you, the hope of glory.

> "My grace is sufficient for thee, for my power
> shows up best in weak people."
> **II Corinthians 12:9**

This wonderful miracle given to me reminds me of a song by Doug Jordan which has been such an encouragement and blessing to me. I would like to share it with you. Perhaps you've heard it before.

> Don't give up on the brink of a miracle
> Don't give in God is still on the throne
> Don't give up on the brink of a miracle
> Don't give up, remember you're not alone

The power and consequences of Christ victory has now engulfed me or as the great Martin Luther King Jr. so eloquently stated it:

"FREE AT LAST, FREE AT LAST, PRAISE GOD ALMIGHTY I'M FREE AT LAST!

Chapter 10

Waiting with Three Angels for the Rapture

Ecclesiastes 3:1 To everything there is a season and a purpose under heaven:

By now, as you have seen and learned, I had become pretty familiar with my new friend who was guiding me and leading me through my new Book. After the wonderful experience, I have shared with you I began to ask myself, why was this glorious revelation of the love and power of Jesus Christ given to me? What purpose was it to serve? Could the knowledge I gained in my search be a help to others?

I had read in my book, scriptures that pointed to a teaching taught in the churches known as the rapture. Scriptures such as:

I Corinthians 15: 51,52
51 Behold, I shew you a mystery; We shall not all sleep, but we shall all be changed,
52 In a moment, in the twinkling of an eye, at the last trump: for the trumpet shall sound, and the dead shall be raised incorruptible, and we shall be changed.
I Thessalonians 4:16-18 For the Lord himself shall descend from heaven with a shout, with the voice of the archangel, and with the trump of God: and the dead in Christ shall rise first:
17 Then we which are alive and remain shall be caught up together with them in the clouds, to meet the Lord in the air: and so shall we ever be with the Lord.
18 Wherefore comfort one another with these words.

Yet being intellectually honest with myself, a question crossed my mind, "Is this true, what is being taught in the churches today about the Rapture? Specifically that we will be raptured out of this evil world before the period of the great tribulation and the return of Christ?. Then what is the purpose or necessity of preparing ourselves for that event? Since we will be changed then and be translated at that event, why trouble myself with making a translation preparation?

Christ, Himself has warned us *"Therefore be ye also ready: for in such an hour that ye think not the Son of man cometh."*
Matthew 24: 44

Those scriptures and questions about those verses bring me to the one of the purposes I outlined in the preface and purpose of this book.

This testimony is an attempt to help those who profess to be followers of Jesus Christ, to make a translation preparation as we travel to the Heavenly Promised Land and to the Celestial City.

In attempting to find the answer to these questions in biblical terms, my ignorance in regards to with this issue cost me many additional years of demonic oppressive captivity. Therefore understanding the translation preparation is vital to our present and future welfare.

While I continued reading and studying my new Book, the Lord led me to another discovery. It was the story of the three angels. Have you yet heard the story about the three angels in your personal journey to the Celestial City?

It goes something like this:

> **Revelation 14: 6-11** And I saw another angel fly in the midst of heaven, having the everlasting gospel to preach unto them that dwell on the earth, and to every nation, and kindred, and tongue, and people,
> 7 Saying with a loud voice, Fear God, and give glory to him; for the hour of his judgment is come: and worship him that made heaven, and earth, and the sea, and the fountains of waters.
> 8 And there followed another angel, saying, Babylon is fallen, is fallen, that great city because she made all nations drink of the wine of the wrath of her fornication.
> 9 And the third angel followed them, saying with a loud voice, If any man worship the beast and his image, and receive his mark in his forehead, or in his hand,
> 10 The same shall drink of the wine of the wrath of God, which is poured out without mixture into the cup of his indignation; and he shall be tormented with fire and brimstone in the presence of the holy angels, and in the presence of the Lamb:
> 11 And the smoke of their torment ascendeth up forever and ever: and they have no rest day nor night, who worship the beast and his image, and whosoever receiveth the mark of his name.

Now that first angel's everlasting gospel message I had no trouble with, for as I have shared it with you by my testimony. Our gracious Lord and Savior had cleansed me from the guilt and power of my sins. What a wonderful Savior is Jesus my Savior, what a wonderful Savior is Jesus, my Lord! Have you ever heard that song before? How about this song, perhaps you have experienced this one?

> What can wash away my sins?
> Nothing but the blood of Jesus
> What can make me whole again?
> Nothing but the blood of Jesus

> Oh precious is that flow
> That makes me white as snow
> Tis' the only font I know
> Nothing but the blood of Jesus

The second angel didn't pose too much problem for me, for I perhaps, like you had heard from Bible teachers preaching and teaching numerous times about a corrupt church in this last day generation.

However, now this third angel had a message that also captured my attention along with my thankfulness of the good news of the everlasting gospel of that first one. I'll have more to say on this angel later.

I knew even as a young boy when I heard stories about fire and brimstone, that wasn't a place I cared to be. The place that Christ has prepared, one that He calls Heaven is where I want to be, how about you?

By the way, have you decided where you would like to end up when this thing of sin and rebellion is all over?

Yes me too!

This business about *the wine of the wrath of God* being poured out without any mingling of His mercy captured my curiosity. If the books I had read like Hal Lindsey's "The Late Great Planet Earth, Thomas Ice and Randall Price's 'Ready to Rebuild'" and the videos I had viewed like Peter and Paul Lalonde's "Left Behind" and "Tribulation" were Biblically true, then there would be no need for a translation preparation.

I have no need for concern, for I would be "snatched up" standing before God when He pours out His wrath in the great tribulation. If I didn't manage to hold onto my salvation, freely given to me in Christ, or if I procrastinated with my decision to follow Christ, then no problem. Even though I would have a rough time of it, I will be given a second chance according to this teaching.

By the way, these Rapture stories had a familiar ring to them, they kind of remind me of the stories I had heard as a young boy while in Catholic School. The nuns also taught me that I would be given another chance to make Heaven if I missed this one in this life, in a place called Purgatory. Have you ever heard of that place? It's not in Scripture. I know I've checked. Have you?

In contrast to these teachings, I read in my new Book stories that Jesus taught like the story of the Ten Virgins. Ten girls professing to have pure faith and *preparation made to receive the bridegroom.*

Matthew 25:1-13 Then shall the kingdom of heaven be likened unto ten virgins, which took their lamps and went forth to meet the bridegroom.
2 And five of them were wise, and five were foolish.
3 They that were foolish took their lamps, and took no oil with them:
4 But the wise took oil in their vessels with their lamps.
5 While the bridegroom tarried, they all slumbered and slept.
6 And at midnight there was a cry made, Behold, the bridegroom cometh; go ye out to meet him.
7 Then all those virgins arose and trimmed their lamps.
8 And the foolish said unto the wise, Give us of your oil; for our lamps are gone out.
9 But the wise answered, saying, Not so; lest there be not enough for us and you: but go ye rather to them that sell, and buy for yourselves.

10 And while they went to buy, the bridegroom came; and *they that were ready* went in with him to the marriage: and the door was shut.
11 Afterward came also the other virgins, saying, Lord, Lord, open to us.
12 But he answered and said, Verily I say unto you, I know you not.
13 Watch, therefore, for ye know neither the day nor the hour wherein the Son of man cometh.

The point of this wonderful story *is the preparation that has to made in this life* before the bridegroom (symbolizing Christ) returns. Behold, the bridegroom cometh. Go ye out to meet him, and *they that were ready* went in with him to the marriage:

I also read in the book of Malachi the prophecy of the people of God living in the last days before Jesus Christ returns to this earth.

Malachi 3: 1-3 Behold, I will send my messenger, and he shall prepare the way before me: and the Lord, whom ye seek, shall suddenly come to his temple, even the messenger of the covenant, whom ye delight in: behold, he shall come, saith the Lord of hosts.
2 But who may abide the day of his coming? and who shall stand when he appeareth? for he is like a refiner's fire, and like fullers' soap:
3 And he shall sit as a refiner and purifier of silver: and he shall purify the sons of Levi, and purge them as gold and silver, that they may offer unto the Lord an offering in righteousness.

As shared with you earlier that in the terrible condition I found myself in, I certainly wasn't in a position, which could be illustrated as refined as gold or silver, or cleansed like fuller's soap (from demonic filthiness), to be an offering unto the Lord.

Romans 12:1-2 I beseech you therefore, brethren, by the mercies of God, that ye present your bodies a living sacrifice, holy, acceptable unto God, which is your reasonable service.
2 And be not conformed to this world: but be ye transformed by the renewing of your mind, that ye may prove what is that good, and acceptable, and perfect, will of God.

These words burned like fire in my heart for they were answering a longing and thirst in my soul that would not be quenched. That desire was to be liberated from the power and consequences of sin which tormented my mind, soul, and life. I longed to posses the experience those ten girls had, to present myself as an offering in righteousness, holiness, and acceptance unto God—to be ready to go into the marriage feast. However, *that presented a dilemma. I didn't possess the power or the ability to accomplish such an achievement.*

The Lord had to teach me over a period of twenty-three years, that without Christ and His Sovereign power, I could nothing for or toward His glory and honor—absolutely NOTHING. "O" As you will again recall.

John 15:4,5 Abide in me, and I in you. As the branch cannot bear fruit of itself, except it abide in the vine; no more can ye, except ye abide in me.
5 I am the vine, ye are the branches: He that abideth in me, and I in him, the same bringeth forth much fruit: *for without me ye can do nothing.*

Yet despite my unworthiness, helplessness, and trouble, I clung tenaciously to His promise found in my new Book. It was to become one of my all-time favorites.

Psalm 32: 7 *Thou art my hiding place; thou shalt preserve me from trouble; thou shalt compass me about with songs of deliverance.*

The companion text following it also brought me great comfort.

Psalm 32: 8 I will instruct thee and teach thee in the way which thou shalt go: I will guide thee with mine eye.

I certainly did need some assurance, in light of the way I had messed up my life thus far. As I continued to read and study about this translation business, the Lord led me to some very interesting promises. They are what I will call translation preparation promises.

II Corinthians 7:1 Having therefore these promises, dearly beloved, let us cleanse ourselves from all filthiness of the flesh and spirit, perfecting holiness in the fear of God.

Here are a few more:

Isaiah 54:17 *No weapon that is formed against thee shall prosper*, and every tongue that shall rise against thee in judgment thou shalt condemn. This is the heritage of the servants of the Lord, and their righteousness is of me, saith the Lord.
Psalm 56:9 When I cry unto thee, then shall mine enemies turn back: this I know; for *God is for me.*
Luke 10:19 Behold, I give unto you power to tread on serpents and scorpions and over all the power of the enemy: and nothing shall by any means hurt you. (This is a really important one!)
II Corinthians 10:4,5 For the weapons of our warfare are not carnal, but mighty through God to the pulling down of strongholds.
5 Casting down imaginations, and every high thing that exalteth itself against the knowledge of God, and *bringing into captivity every thought to the obedience of Christ.*

By our Heavenly Father's love and by the Sovereignty of the Lord Jesus Christ and through the agency of the Holy Spirit, He gave us these powerful promises. He enabled me to gain the victory and dominance over the power of sin and Satan that was destroying my welfare, my happiness, and my life. He gave me a desire to be like those ten girls that presented their bodies a living sacrifice as an offering *by Christ's righteousness*, acceptable unto God. (by faith alone as I shared earlier in my testimony)

    Being armed with these glorious promises must be akin to Prudence, Piety, and Charity, showing Christian those wonderful engines that other servants of God had accomplished wonderful things with. Such as Moses rod, the hammer and nail that Jael slew Sisera with, the pitchers, trumpets, and lamps that Gideon used to put to flight the armies of Midian. The jaw-bone that Samson used to fight the Philistines; David's sling that he used to slay the giant Goliah of Gath and the sword that the Lord will use to kill the Man of Sin.

    However Christian had to continue his journey after being shown all these wonderful treasures and I too must continue on my way with my story and journey.

Chapter 11

Victory in Christ—So What's the Problem?

Since it is both biblically and experientially true that the translation preparation of the living has to occur before Jesus comes, I discovered that Christ has a real problem. Would you like to know what it is?

Well in my study of my new Book Christ led me to discover:
1. Jesus Christ is our High Priest.
Hebrews 8:1 Now of the things which we have spoken this is the sum: We have such a high priest, who is set on the right hand of the throne of the Majesty in the heavens;
2. Jesus Christ carries us on His great heart of love before His Father in the heavenly sanctuary.
Hebrews 9:24 For Christ is not entered into the holy places made with hands, which are the figures of the true; but into heaven itself, now to appear in the presence of God for us.
3. Jesus Christ bore the penalty of our sins and transgressions against the Sacred Law of God.
Isaiah 53:3-6 He is despised and rejected of men; a man of sorrows, and acquainted with grief: and we hid as it were our faces from him; he was despised, and we esteemed him not.
4 Surely he hath borne our griefs and carried our sorrows, yet we did esteem him stricken, smitten of God, and afflicted.
5 But *he was wounded for our transgressions*; he was bruised for our iniquities. The chastisement of our peace was upon him, and with his stripes, we are healed.
6 We are like sheeps that have gone astray; we have turned every one to his own way; *and the Lord hath laid on him the iniquity of us all.*
John 3:16 *For God so loved the world, that he gave his only begotten Son, that whosoever believeth in him should not perish, but have everlasting life.*

I John 3:4 Whosoever committeth sin transgresseth also the law: for sin is the transgression of the law. Which law?

His Father's Law that Christ kept. The same Law Paul and the disciples kept. The Ten Commandments moral law.

John 14:21 He that hath my commandments, and keepeth them, he is that loveth me: and he that loveth me shall be loved of my Father, and I will love him and will manifest myself to him.
John 15:10 If ye keep my commandments, ye shall abide in my love; even as I have kept my Father's commandments, and abide in his love.
Romans 3:21-24,31 But now the righteousness of God without the law is manifested, being witnessed by the law and the prophets;
22 Even the righteousness of God which is by the faith of Jesus Christ unto all and upon all them that believe: for there is no difference:
23 For all have sinned, and come short of the glory of God;
24 Being justified freely by his grace through the redemption that is in Christ Jesus:
31 Do we then make void the law through faith? God forbid: yea, we establish the law.

How does the Lord accomplish such a glorious feat in His people?

Hebrews 8:10 For this is the covenant that I will make with the house of Israel after those days, saith the Lord; I will put my laws into their mind, and write them in their hearts: and I will be to them a God, and they shall be to me a people.
Psalm 40:8 I delight to do thy will, O my God: yea, thy law is within my heart.
Psalm 119:97,98,105
97 O how love I thy law! it is my meditation all day.

98 Thou through thy commandments hast made me wiser than mine enemies: for they are ever with me.

105 Thy word is a lamp unto my feet and a light unto my path.

Colossians 1:26,27

26 Even the mystery which hath been hidden from ages and generations, but now is made manifest to his saints:

27 To whom God would make known what is the riches of the glory of this mystery among the Gentiles; which is Christ in you, the hope of glory.

Christ living in us revealing His glory has to have a people ready for translation when He comes the second time unto salvation. That's the whole purpose of our translation preparation.

Speaking of the preparation for our translation, I will expand on this in more detail in chapter 12, A Personal Message, and Concern from Dan.

The following little parable will illustrate what I'm trying to say to you.

Let's imagine a clandestine (secret) meeting called by Satan, the great adversary himself.

He has gathered all his fallen angels around him and here is what he says to them: "Remember how we were cast out of heaven for our rebellion in transgressing the will of God and His commandments." Recall also how we lost our battle at Calvary because we couldn't get Christ to violate His Father's will. "Well, I'm convinced *we can win this controversy with God* before Christ returns to the earth with His rewards." Satan's evil angels ask, "how can we do that?"

Satan says, "here's what I want you to do. I want you to go out into all the earth and bring pressure to bear on every Christian who professes to love and serve Jesus Christ."

"Use whatever means it takes, but keep them breaking God's commandments and prevent them from obtaining a preparation for translation. *Then if Christ should translate one Christian without seeing death when He returns, who is not in obedience to the will of God Christ will have to take me and all the rest of you back into Heaven as well."*

You know I think there's not an honest judge alive, who wouldn't argue that Satan would have a valid case that would hold up in court.

You see Satan's life and personal existence depend upon his ability to prevent a people from being in the position of living in the center of God's will and keeping His commandments when Christ comes to deliver His people from this sin-cursed world.

Revelation 14:12 *Here is the patience of the saints: here are they that keep the commandments of God, and the faith of Jesus.*

Being in the center of God's will and the keeping of His commandments is what the preparation for translation is all about (more on this later as I said).

Just as King Nebuchadnezzar did, Satan is determined to rob God's glory and power that is contained in His Word that is given to us freely by God. *We can't earn it and we are unworthy to receive it, yet Christ gives it to us as a gift.* Not understanding this caused me to live in spiritual darkness and mental illness for so many additional years.

II Corinthians 4:4 *In whom the god of this world hath blinded the minds of them which believe not,* lest the light of the glorious gospel of Christ, who is the image of God, should shine unto them.

So before Christ comes back, we must be in the center of God's will, having received Christ's righteousness. Or we will not receive our new glorified bodies, but instead will be destroyed by the brightness of His coming along with the living wicked.

II Thessalonians 2:8 And then shall that Wicked be revealed, whom the Lord shall consume with the spirit of his mouth, and shall destroy with the brightness of his coming.

Can you see why this glorious revelation of the love and power of Jesus Christ is given to us? What purpose it is to serve?

Psalm 119: 9-12,97,98,105
9 Wherewithal shall a young man cleanse his way? by taking heed thereto according to thy word.
10 With my whole heart have I sought thee: O let me not wander from thy commandments.
11 *Thy word have I hid in mine heart, that I might not sin against thee.*
12 Blessed art thou, O Lord: teach me thy statutes.
97 *O how love I thy law!* it is my meditation all day.
98 Thou through thy commandments hast made me wiser than mine enemies: for they are ever with me.
105 *Thy word is a lamp unto my feet and a light unto my path.*

Revelation 12:11, 14:12
12:11 And they overcame him by the blood of the Lamb, and by the word of their testimony, and they loved not their lives unto the death.
14:12 Here is the patience of the saints: here are they that keep the commandments of God, and the faith of Jesus.

You see Christ's followers must be brought into translation preparation before He comes. *That's Christ's problem and challenge, in preparing His people who would rather die than to be disloyal to the One whom has shown them so much kindness and with who He has shared so much of His goodness and love,*

Let me put it in another way.

If I take out of my Bible everything that men wrote such as Isaiah, Jeremiah, Amos, Obadiah, Jonah, who are they anyway, they are just men.

I also remove, say, Matthew, Mark, Luke, John—they are also are just men after all. So after I remove everything that men have written, what do I have left?

I'm left with the Ten Commandments because they were not written by a man. They were written by God's own finger on two tablets of stone.

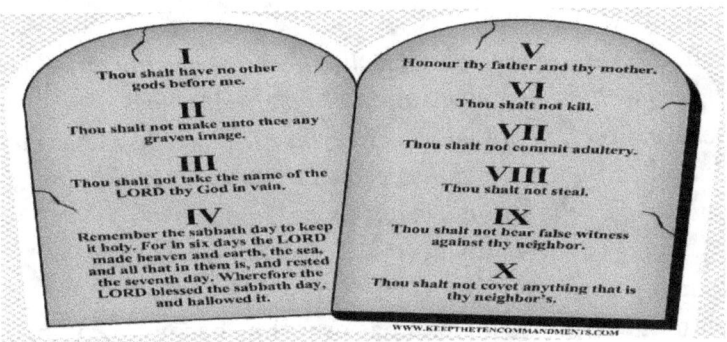

The only thing in God's good book that He could not trust men to write, was the Ten Commandments. Men couldn't write them for they had just disobeyed them (remember the golden calf debacle).

So then I begin to examine those Ten Commandments and I read:

Thou shalt not kill

Thou shalt not commit adultery

Thou shalt not steal

Thou shalt not bear false witness

Then I stiffen up my neck and I rare back shaking my fist to God and I say "By what authority do you have to tell me what I can do or what I can't do.

The answer comes softly back, "I made you, you are the child of my creation."

Genesis 1:27 So God created man in His own image; in the image of God He created him, male and female He created them.

Exodus 20:11 For in six days the Lord made heaven and earth, the sea, and all that in them is, and rested the seventh day, wherefore the Lord blessed the Sabbath day, and hallowed it.

So this is where God gets His authority over His children that He created. I ask you, "is there any parent with children who doesn't understand that? So it is rational to believe that if God has an enemy (and we know who that is) it only makes sense that God's enemy would attack God's authority, and try to undermine that authority, and would do it to get God's people to break God's law and to defy that authority.
I repeat, can *you see that Christ's followers must be brought into translation preparation, to prepare a people before He comes. That's Christ's problem and challenge, to prepare a people who would rather die than be disloyal to the One who has shown them so much kindness, love, and mercy and with whom He has shared so much of His goodness.*

There's a text in my new Book that was given to me by a godly nurse many years ago, and then years later, another godly woman gave it to me in music form. It has over time become very special to me. From that summer of 1970 when I had my mental breakdown to the writing of this book, it kind of sums up this whole forty-seven-year experience for me.

Psalm 40:1-3 I waited patiently for the Lord: and He inclined unto me, and heard my cry.
2 He brought me up also out of a horrible pit, out of the miry clay, and set my feet upon a rock, and established my goings.
3 And He hath put a new song in my mouth, even praise unto our God, many shall see it, and fear, and trust in the Lord.

Although blinded by the world's deceptions and raised as a young boy in a pool hall and tavern, without a knowledge of God, and turning his back on spiritual matters, going to war and in the process of losing his sanity; finally by God's sovereign grace and infinite mercy, he came to know his heavenly Father and Jesus Christ in whom He has sent and possess's this relationship which is eternal life, He has put a new song in my mouth! Even praise unto our God is what I want to give Jesus Christ in witnessing and testifying to you, and as you can now see for yourself, *I have a lot to testify to.*

- I testify to having a desire to be ready for Jesus to come in light of the glorious revelation of the Preparation for Translation.
- I testify to the message of the Three Angels.
- I testify to having a desire to come out of the darkness of ignorance and deception and to come into the light by being prepared for translation and rejecting the notion that I will be given another chance of salvation after the Rapture.
- I testify to the truth of Christ writing His Father's Law of the New Covenant in my mind and my heart.
- I testify to the truth and the realization that of myself I did not possess the power, strength, or ability to accomplish the task of gaining the victory over any destructive aspect of my life.
- I testify that despite the ongoing attacks from the enemy and despite my unworthiness, it is Jesus Christ by the agency of the Holy Spirit and the power of His Holy Word that has given me the victory. Victory over Satan's control over my life of rebellion, alcohol, tobacco, addictions and the pain from a broken life, and despair which caused the attempt of taking of my life.
- I testify to the Lord Jesus Christ for blessing me with His grace and power that enabled me to give my testimony in this little book and the ability to share it with you.
- I testify to the truth, as it is in Christ Jesus, that "if you have faith and doubt not." And shall say unto the mountain of demonic oppression and possession, "be thou removed and be cast into the sea;" and doubt not but believe; then those things which thou saith shall come to pass. You shall have whatsoever you saith. Therefore I say unto you, "whatsoever you desire, when you pray, believe that you have received them, and you shall have them." **Mark 11: 22-24**

• I testify that I choose to make myself available for Christ for His use in defeating His archenemy in his continued attempt to rob God's Word of its power, *authority*, and glory freely given to His children by and in Christ Jesus.

• I testify to what great things the Lord has done for me! EVEN PRAISE UNTO OUR GOD!

Revelation 5:11-13 And I beheld, and I heard the voice of many angels round about the throne and the beasts and the elders: and the number of them was ten thousand times ten thousand, and thousands of thousands;

12 Saying with a loud voice, Worthy is the Lamb that was slain to receive power, and riches, and wisdom, and strength, and honour, and glory, and blessing.

13 And every creature which is in heaven, and on the earth, and under the earth, and such as are in the sea, and all that are in them, heard I saying, *"Blessing, and honour, and glory, and power, be unto Him that sitteth upon the throne, and unto the Lamb forever and ever."*

Chapter 12

A Personal Message and Concern from Dan

These last three chapters contains a message from our Loving and Sovereign God of all creation. I bear a personal responsibility to share it with you at the peril of my own eternal salvation if I don't. It is a mandate from the courts of Heaven given in mercy and love from our Heavenly Father to me, despite my unworthiness, to give to those whom He loves, as He loves as His own Son Jesus Christ. May the Lord add His blessing and favor upon the final chapters of this book. The following is the mandate:

Ezekiel 3:4,17-21
4 And he said unto me, Son of man, go, get thee unto the house of Israel, (those that claim Jesus Christ as their Lord and King) and speak with My words unto them.
17 Son of man, I have made thee a watchman unto the house of Israel: therefore hear the word at my mouth, and give them warning from me.
18 When I say unto the wicked, Thou shalt surely die; and thou givest him not warning, nor speakest to warn the wicked from his wicked way, to save his life; the same wicked man shall die in his iniquity, but his blood will I require at thine hand.
19 Yet if thou warn the wicked, and he turns not from his wickedness, nor from his wicked way, he shall die in his iniquity; but thou hast delivered thy soul.
20 Again, When a righteous man doth turn from his righteousness, and commit iniquity, and I lay a stumbling block before him, he shall die: *because thou hast not given him a warning, he shall die in his sin, and his righteousness which he hath done shall not be remembered; but his blood will I require at thine hand.*

21 *Nevertheless if thou warn the righteous man, that the righteous sin not, and he doth not sin, he shall surely live, because he is warned; also thou hast delivered thy soul.*

In those intervening years after my wonderful deliverance from the evil powers arrayed against me, it has taken many years to recuperate (I am still in that process of healing. I walk with a mental limp, my broken vessel, if you will, as shared earlier— PTSD and chronic headaches from what I believe is caused by my exposure to agent orange in the war). I had done physical damage to my body and my brain from the many year's misuses of mind-altering medications. During this recovery time, the Lord revealed another life-altering revelation to me as I kept reading and studying my new Book. It caused me grave concern, for it too held consequences which had adversely affected my life and had a hand in bringing me into that fearful condition I have shared with you in such detail.

What follows is that life-altering revelation the Lord has revealed and that causes me such great concern for His people.
I am concerned about what the churches are teaching in regard to the prophecies of Matthew 24, Daniel 7, 8 and 9 and the book of Revelation. These great end-time prophecies also hold the key to the glorious task of translation preparation.

You see these wonderful prophecies are interpreted by one of two prophetic systems or models if you prefer that terminology.

Moses laid down the first system. All the other writers of the Bible, including Paul, adopted the same model of interpretation. This was also the view adopted by Martin Luther and was used by him in the mighty Reformation of the Church in the 1500s.

Luther's view regarding the vision of the evil beast of Revelation 13 is as follows:
- That the beast with its mark was active in the past, (at the time of Paul).
- That beast is *active in the present*, (at the time of Luther).
- That the beast of Revelation 13 *will be active in the fut*ure (during our time) right up until the time of Christ's return.

Because of the views of Luther and other reformation Father's, such as Wesley and Calvin thousands of people left the

Catholic Church and helped form many of the Protestant churches we know of today.

The Roman Catholic leadership became alarmed by the acceptance of this system of interpretation of the Scriptures by the common people. The Catholic leadership through the sect of the Jesuits attempted to head off the crisis by assigning a Jesuit priest named Francisco Ribera to develop a second system of interpretation to cancel out the force of this Protestant Reformation. The counter-reformation was enacted to counteract this new Protestant movement.

So in the 1500s, 1580 to be precise, the Jesuit priest Ribera wrote his book with a different view and interpretation of the teachings of prophecies expounded by the Protestants. The Roman Church promoted it, and as a result, it effectively stopped the Reformation in its tracks and won back the Balken States of Europe to the Catholic Church.

Would you like to know what the Jesuits taught?

- They taught that the beast of Revelation 13 w*as not active in the past, was not active in the present, and will not be active until the end of the age.*
- They also taught that the Jews would be converted at the end of the age.
- That the Jews were the remnant and that the Jews would encounter the beast and the antichrist and that it would be the Jews who would know what the mark of the beast is, and would be able to identify the image of the beast.
- Ribera reinterpreted Revelation chapters 4 through 18 and taught that they would not be fulfilled until the end of the age in the far distant future.

"Thus in Ribera's commentary was laid the foundation for that great structure of Futurism, built upon and enlarged by those who followed, until it became the common Catholic position.

And then, a wonder of wonders, in the nineteenth century this Jesuit scheme of interpretation came to be adopted by a growing

number of Protestants, until today Futurism, amplified and adorned with the Rapture theory, has become the generally accepted belief of the Fundamentalist wing of popular Protestantism."
(LeRoy Edwin Froom, The Prophetic Faith of Our Fathers Vol.II page 493)

You may be wondering when this end of the age time would begin?

In Scotland in the 1830s, in a Protestant Church called the Plymouth Brethren Church of Glasgow, a woman by the name of Margaret McDonald went into a vision. She reported that it had been told her in the vision that Christ could come that night and catch up His people secretly.

The following is a quote from a Christian radio newsman who authored a book on Margaret McDonald.

"Several observations are in order:

First of all, she evidently did not believe in imminence; she thought that "the fullness of Christ" (Spirit-filling) was first necessary, "and then shall we be caught up to meet him."
She said that the catching up (or Rapture) would be seen only by Spirit-filled believers—a secret coming." *(The Incredible Cover-Up, Exposing the Origins of Rapture Theories, Dave MacPherson forward by* Dr. James McKeever, page 154)

Margaret McDonald in effect supported and verified the teachings of the Jesuit priest Riberia three hundred years earlier, that the Rapture would occur at the end of the age. The end of the age is the end of the great three and one half year tribulation after the covenant has been broken with the Jews by the Anti-Christ of Daniel 7:25. The Anti-Christ who breaks God's covenant will be the one standing upon the temple mount on the old city of Jerusalem in the state of Israel.

This is a false interpretation of Scripture by a Jesuit priest and supported by visions using this wrong model of interpretation of the Scriptures.

Revelation 22:18,19

18 For I testify unto every man that heareth the words of the prophecy of this book If any man shall add unto these things, God shall add unto him the plagues that are written in this book: **19** And if any man shall take away from the words of the book of this prophecy, God shall take away his part out of the book of life, and out of the holy city, and from the things which are written in this book.

I began to understand how dangerous this deceptive teaching really is *because what if this interpretation of prophecy is incorrect?* If it is incorrect, it would have far-reaching implications.

You see, this interpretation *historically had stopped the Reformation* in Europe. That was then, but what about today? Since I personally believe that I am a member of the last generation, historically speaking, *I could be being deceived now!* Not only that, but in the future, I could unwittingly help enforce the mark of the beast while I'm thinking I'm following the will of God, and *lose my salvation in the process.* That's pretty serious business to me.

In effect, the Catholic Church Theologians and a decision by the National Council of Churches adopted the theory of the Secret Rapture that took away many of the prophecies of the book of Revelation from the last generation.

Now many thousands of Christians are waiting and watching for the Jewish nation to be converted and the end of the age to commence. And I believe that I am not only historically but also personally a part of the last generation. Therefore the Catholic Church has effectively taken chapters 4 through 18 of the book of Revelation away from me.

On a broader scale, every practicing Protestant and Catholic could also be deceived without even knowing it.

I'll explain what I'm trying to say with the following illustration:

In Christ's day, there were also two systems of interpretations of the prophecies of the coming of the Messiah.

Remember when Christ rode into Jerusalem on that small donkey.

Recall all the excitement of the people as they waved palm branches and laid down their cloaks for His entry into the gates. The people in their excitement thought that Christ was riding into Jerusalem to take David's throne, set up His kingdom, and finally defeat the hated Romans.

They had been taught by their religious teachers to expect and to look for a great military and political leader like King David to take possession of David's throne.

Remember to the bitter disappointment of His followers as they experienced all their hopes die with Christ's death upon the cross. Poor Peter really had a rough time for not only did he end up denying that Christ was the Messiah; he denied he even knew the man.

The reason for that faith trying experience and the bitterness of disappointed hopes was the fact that the majority of the people believed the system of interpretation of the prophecies regarding the Messiah that had been taught to them from their youth. It was a *spiritual deception* that the Messiah would reign in power upon David's throne and break the Roman yoke of oppression from off His chosen people.

In contrast with the majority of the people under this delusion, there was a minority of the people (like John the Baptist) that believed in an alternative interpretation of the messianic prophecies. That the Messiah would suffer as the smitten and forsaken Lamb of God.

Those who held to the view of the reigning king interpretation actually crucified their Savior and Messiah saying to Him, "come down from the cross and we will believe."

Those people lost their lives, their city, and their covenant with God! Remember our Lord sorrowfully saying to them, "you know not the time of your visitation…and your house is left unto you desolate". In 70 AD, Christ's prophetic words were fulfilled when the Roman General Titus destroyed the city of Jerusalem.

Christ didn't say to them, "you're mixed up in your interpretation of prophecy." He said to them "your house is left unto you desolate." In other words, you have chosen to throw it all away, and you have lost it all. (Excerpted from What to Say in a Whole New Way, by Daniel W. O'Fill with Johnson Shewmake, copyright 1994 by Review and Herald Publishing Association)

Can you see how dangerous a spiritual deception is?
**Being alert when prophecy is being fulfilled
is a matter of life and death!**

In reviewing my life and my personal covenant relationship with God I recognized that I too had not been alert to the time of my visitation and the prophecies being fulfilled in my life, missing the prophecies for the last generation in the Book of Revelation; missing all those years of the time of my visitation, missing the experience of preparation for translation with my Creator and friend and trading a relationship with Him for a job in a pool hall.

(I suppose I should at this point define what I believe is the preparation for translation. It is not perfection, but a turning away from rebellion against God and His government to loyalty to God and His government)

For you see the life-changing revelation of the necessity of a preparation for translation, and the spiritual deception of a false interpretation of the Scriptures had contributed dramatically to the tragic outcome of my life. I like King Nebuchadnezzar was *experiencing a serious and deadly spiritual condition as a result of this serious and dangerous spiritual deception* and my own foolish choices.

In the tragic and destructive path I had chosen as a result of being spiritually blinded, I was experiencing the full force and impact of the Roman Church's teaching through the Jesuit Priest's and the Protestant Church's embracing of it in modern time.

In light of all that has happened in my life and as a result of learning this information I was faced with the question of which prophetic interpretation to accept as the governing agency in my life. I was faced with two alternatives.

First: If the Catholic Ribera and the Protestant Margaret McDonald were correct, then by accepting their teachings I would be joining them in their ideology of teaching that the Jews would be the people who would accomplish Christ's goal. That lofty goal of being the commandment-keeping people possessing the faith of Jesus brought into translation preparation during the end of the age.

Therefore as a non-Jew I wouldn't have to be immediately concerned about preparing myself for translation at Christ's Second Coming. I could have reasoned that there was no urgency to that preparation, for if I missed this opportunity I would be given another chance after the Rapture, during the Great Tribulation. Then sometime in the future while being blinded by this spiritual deception, I would risk, because of that deception, helping enforce the mark of the beast, all the while thinking I was doing God's will; *the result being, placing my eternal salvation in jeopardy and risk being lost in the process.*

Can you begin to hear the voice of the third angel getting louder? Can you see that the Papacy with its counterpart the Vatican with its order of Jesuits as those responsible for changing the Word of God to include a false teaching on the Rapture?

> **Revelation 22:19** And if any man shall take away from the words of the book of this prophecy, God shall take away his part out of the book of life, and out of the holy city, and from the things that are written in this book.

Second: I could accept Luther's system of interpretation of the last day prophecies, that the beast was active in the past, is here now, and will be active until Jesus comes. I could choose to become one of the participants during this end time that actively collaborates with Christ now in accomplishing His goal of bringing His people into translation preparation. I could choose to be one of those remnant people of which is prophesied: "who will keep the commandments of God and have the faith of Jesus and *follow the lamb wherever He leads.*" Revelation 14:12, 4. This is what I have chosen to do.

Revelation 14:4,12
4… These are they which follow the Lamb whithersoever he goeth.
12 Here is the patience of the saints: here are they that keep the commandments of God, and the faith of Jesus.

    I have decided to accept Luther's historical model of interpretation of these prophecies and to raise my voice in warning against the beast and his image, to witness to the *danger of believing this spiritual deception* (by the writing of this book).
    By the grace and mighty power of the Great Sovereign God and King of the Universe, all the demons of hell have not been able to prevent me from the writing and publishing of this book of my personal testimony.
    Because I have, like King Nebuchadnezzar, felt and experienced the full force and impact of believing a false spiritual teaching which resulted in a fearful and dangerous condition, of which except by the grace and mercy of God I would not have survived.
    On the other hand, I have also experienced the glorious and liberating joy and freedom of being delivered from that dangerous deception and condition with its terrible consequences by *faith in and by the power of the blood of the Lord Jesus Christ.*
    My heart trembles at the thought of what this terrible mistake and misunderstanding have cost me personally and what it could cost someone else now or in the future.
    This is why you see I am concerned about what the churches are teaching about Bible prophecy! It dramatically affected my life adversely. Both physically and spiritually on a personal level *and it could adversely affect yours.*

As mentioned earlier and this is vital, therefore I repeat it, *being alert when prophecy is being fulfilled is a matter of life and death!*

This testimony I have shared with you, in this book, is this prophecy in Revelation, which is being fulfilled right before our eyes.

Revelation 22:18,19

18 For I testify unto every man that heareth the words of the prophecy of this book If any man shall add unto these things, God shall add unto him the plagues that are written in this book:

19 And if any man shall take away from the words of the book of this prophecy, God shall take away his part out of the book of life, and out of the holy city, and from the things which are written in this book.

Chapter 13

The Sealing Prophecy

Now we must move on to another aspect of prophecy being fulfilled called "the sealing" because it is part and parcel of the transformation process.

Revelation 7:1-3
1 And after these things I saw four angels standing on the four corners of the earth, holding the four winds of the earth, that the wind should not blow on the earth, nor on the sea, nor on any tree.
2 And I saw another angel ascending from the east, having the seal of the living God: and he cried with a loud voice to the four angels, to whom it was given to hurt the earth and the sea,
3 Saying, Hurt not the earth, neither the sea nor the trees, *till we have sealed the servants of our God in their foreheads.*
Revelation 22:4 And they shall see his face, and *his name shall be in their foreheads.*
Revelation 14:1 And I looked, and, lo, a Lamb stood on the mount Sion, and with him a hundred forty and four thousand, having his Father's name written in their foreheads.

Before I proceed any further, I wish to make a disclaimer at this point. I am not laying claim of being one of the 144,000. I do, however, desire with all my heart to make a preparation for translation that those chosen blessed ones will have to make to meet our Lord without seeing death, at His second coming. (I have already explained what I believe that preparation is; loyalty to God and His government).

The prophecy is clear enough. The servants of God will be sealed with the Father's Name written in their foreheads. I will not be here, at this place in my book, attempting to prove that our Heavenly Father's name is Yahweh, God, or Jehovah. Scholars much brighter than I have written volumes on the subject.

However, I just want to say at this point that I have chosen to believe and accept that *His personal name is* the Hebrew rendition of *Yahweh*. What name you choose to use is between you and God. In addition to all the titles attributed to Him. I believe based upon scripture and my personal experience if you have accepted Jesus Christ as your personal Lord and Savior, in the born again New Covenant experience, and have a true living relationship with the Lord Jesus Christ, then you have the Father's name written upon your heart (in your forehead).

John 10: 30 I am my Father are one.
Matthew 10: 40 He that receives you receiveth me, and he that receiveth me receiveth Him that sent me.
The seal of God is of course in direct contrast to those who receive the mark of the beast in their forehead or in their hand.
Revelation 13:16,17
16 And he causeth all, both small and great, rich and poor, free and bond, to receive a mark in their right hand, or their foreheads:
17 And that no man might buy or sell, save *he that had the mark, or the name of the beast, or the number of his name.*

When it gets down to the very end there are only going to be two groups. Only two! Those will be your only options to choose from.

One group the mark of the beast, the other group the seal of God. Have you figured out which group you want to be in yet? I have and it's the group with the seal of God written in my forehead (whatever I understand His name to be.) Not a mark stamped on it!

Speaking of visible marks, have you ever wondered what it is that will be in our foreheads? A label with UPC Bar codes perhaps? RFID chips perhaps? Have you ever considered the symbolic nature of the book of Revelation?

EXODUS 20

1. And God spake all these words, saying,
2. I am the Lord thy God, which have brought thee out of the land of Egypt, out of the house of bondage.
3. Thou shalt have no other gods before me.
4. Thou shalt not make unto thee any graven image or any likeness of anything that is in heaven above, or that is in the earth beneath, or that is in the water under the earth:
5. Thou shalt not bow down thyself to them, nor serve them: for I the Lord thy God am a jealous God, visiting the iniquity of the fathers upon the children unto the third and fourth generation of them that hate me;
6. And shewing mercy unto thousands of them that love me, and keep my commandments.
7. Thou shalt not take the name of the Lord thy God in vain; for the Lord will not hold him guiltless that taketh his name in vain.
8. Remember the sabbath day, to keep it holy.
9. Six days shalt thou labour, and do all thy work:
10. But the seventh day is the sabbath of the Lord thy God: in it, thou shalt not do any work, thou, nor thy son, nor thy daughter, thy manservant, nor thy maidservant, nor thy cattle, nor thy stranger that is within thy gates:
11. For in six days the Lord made heaven and earth, the sea, and all that in them is, and rested the seventh day: wherefore the Lord blessed the sabbath day, and hallowed it.
12. Honour thy father and thy mother: that thy days may be long upon the land which the Lord thy God giveth thee.
13. Thou shalt not kill.
14. Thou shalt not commit adultery.
15. Thou shalt not steal.
16. Thou shalt not bear false witness against thy neighbour.
17. Thou shalt not covet thy neighbour's house, thou shalt not covet thy neighbour's wife, nor his manservant, nor his maidservant, nor his ox, nor his ass, nor anything that is thy neighbour's.

The reason I printed the Ten Commandments in the old Victorian English is that they are so special and meaningful to me. *Right in the middle of that Constitution is the Great Seal of the King of the Universe.*

Exodus 20: 8-11 Remember the Sabbath day, to keep it holy.
9 Six days shalt thou labour, and do all thy work:
10 But the seventh day is the Sabbath of the Lord thy God: in it, thou shalt not do any work, thou, nor thy son, nor thy daughter, thy manservant, nor thy maidservant, nor thy cattle, nor thy stranger that is within thy gates:
For in six days **the Lord made heaven and earth, the sea, and all that in them is,** and rested the seventh day: wherefore the Lord blessed the Sabbath day, and hallowed it.

Can you spot it? The *title of the officeholder and the territory that the officeholder governs.*
The title of the office holder: *the Lord, creator of heaven and earth.*
Which Lord though?

I Corinthians 8:5 For though there be that are called gods, whether in heaven or on earth, as there be gods many, and lords many.

Which Lord makes the claim of being the Creator of the Universe?
John 1:1-3,10,14
1 In the beginning, was the Word, and the Word was with God, and the Word was God.
2 The same was in the beginning with God.
3 *All things were made by him,* and without him was not anything made that was made.
10 He was in the world, and the world was made by him, and the world knew him not.
14 And the *Word was made flesh and dwelt among us,* and we beheld his glory, the glory as of the only begotten of the Father, full of grace and truth.

Well, that pretty narrows it down, doesn't it? The Word who became Jesus Christ is the King of the Universe by virtue of the fact that He created it to begin with; which makes Him the *King of Kings and Lord of Lords!*

Revelation 19: 11-16
11 And I saw heaven opened, and behold a white horse, and he that sat upon him was called Faithful and True, and in righteousness, he doth judge and make war.
12 His eyes were as a flame of fire, and on his head were many crowns; and he had a name written, that no man knew, but he himself.
13 And he was clothed with a vesture dipped in blood: and his name is called The Word of God.
14 And the armies which were in heaven followed him upon white horses, clothed in fine linen, white and clean.
15 And out of his mouth goeth a sharp sword, that with it he should smite the nations: and he shall rule them with a rod of iron: and he treadeth the winepress of the fierceness and wrath of Almighty God.
16 And he hath on his vesture and on his thigh a name is written, *KING OF KINGS, AND LORD OF LORDS.*

Revelation 19: 16 And he hath on his vesture and on his thigh a name is written, *King of Kings and Lord of Lords.*

The territory of which Christ reigns over and governs: heaven and earth, the sea, and all that in them is *The Universe!*

So in this Great Seal of God is found the seal symbolizing the sovereignty and authority of Heaven's government. This seal contains the title of its officeholder and the territory in which the King of the Universe governs. In the center of His Divine Law, the Ten Commandments, which are the foundation of His throne, government, and His domain is the center of His will. Also found there, is the one who holds that office of that Divine government who is *Jesus Christ the Great Creator. Christ bears His Father's name, Yahweh the Word who became known to us as Jesus Christ, and He is King of Kings and Lord of Lords, Creator of the Universe.*

The Great Seal meets the entire criterion. That seal is applied to that document which gives it the power of Heaven's government to back it up with creditability.

Recall the prophecy:

Revelation 7:1-3
1 And after these things I saw four angels standing on the four corners of the earth, holding the four winds of the earth, that the wind should not blow on the earth, nor on the sea, nor on any tree.
2 And I saw another angel ascending from the east, *having the seal of the living God:* and he cried with a loud voice to the four angels, to whom it was given to hurt the earth and the sea,

3 Saying, Hurt not the earth, neither the sea nor the trees, till we have sealed the servants of our God in their foreheads.

Revelation 22:4 And they shall see his face, and *his name shall be in their foreheads.*

Revelation 14:1 And I looked, and, lo, a Lamb stood on the mount Sion, and with him an hundred forty and four thousand, *having his Father's name written in their foreheads.*

The Great Seal of God is clearly seen in His glorious Ten Commandments. Specifically the fourth commandment, that commands our respect and love in calling us to fellowship and worship Him in a sacred time and place. A time and place in which Christ commands His special blessings to be upon His people. A time and place of which His Love is displayed in a manner unique and unrivaled at any other moment in time; *the Seventh Day Sabbath.*

A moment in time where the Son of God, Jesus Christ the wonderful, loving, and magnificent, has placed His Father's signature, YAHWEH, I AM that I AM.

A moment of time sacred to the Creator of Heaven and Earth, which has come under attack and controversy because of another moment of time that, man has put in its place. A time of the first day of the week called Sunday.

That moment that prophecy foretold would come to pass before the end of time. That prophecy is found in the Book of Daniel the prophet. Daniel identifies the one who accomplishes such a sacrilegious feat as changing the times, the laws, and the moments of God.

Daniel 7: 25 And *he shall* speak great words against the most High, and shall wear out the saints of the Most High, and *think to change times and laws*: and they shall be given into his hand until a time and times and the dividing of time. (1260 years)

Chapter 14

The Wonderful Wonder of History

I have arrived at this place in my testimony wherein I have to make a decision. A decision whether or not to share with you an exhaustive Biblical and historical review of prophecy and scripture to prove to you the biblical identity of the persons or organization whom the Word of God identifies as responsible for such a sacrilege mentioned in the previous chapter. Or from the same Word of God and by my testimony, share with you how Jesus Christ and our Heavenly Father feel about this decisive issue. I have chosen the latter for the following reasons.

Over and through the centuries, scholars and theologians regarding this issue have had arguments and debates. In fact, as you may already know, the Protestant movement of the 1500s was born out of such fierce and heated debates.

So my purpose here is not to reargue these issues. It's only to share with you biblically how Christ and His Father feel about this issue and to witness to you through my testimony to what I believe is the truth and how being caught up in this terrible spiritual deception has changed my life.

The books of Daniel and Revelation confront us with these issues, and how deeply God feels about it. As shared earlier, since Christ created all things He created the day of worship. Therefore, He has special feelings about His day of worship. He gives us a special warning of love about its observance. The voices of those three angels just keep getting louder and louder. Can you hear them yet?

Revelation 14:6-10 And I saw another angel fly in the midst of heaven, having the everlasting gospel to preach unto them that dwell on the earth, and to every nation, and kindred, and tongue, and people,
7 Saying with a loud voice, *Fear God, and give glory to him;* for the hour of his judgment is come: and *worship him* that made heaven, and earth, and the sea, and the fountains of waters.
8 And there followed another angel, saying, Babylon is fallen, is fallen, that great city because she made all nations drink of the wine of the wrath of her fornication.
9 And the third angel followed them, saying with a loud voice, *If any man worship the beast and his image,* and receive his mark in his forehead, or in his hand,
10 The same shall drink of the wine of the wrath of God that is poured out without mixture intothe cup of His indignation: and he shall be tormented with fire and brimstone in the presence of the holy angels, and in the presence of the Lamb.

There's the issue right before us, and it appears that the God (Jesus) who created heaven and earth feels strongly about His people, worshiping Him and not the beast or his image.

Now before we get into the issue of worshiping God versus worshiping the beast, (which as you will see is a governmental power that attempts to change God's laws) for now I would like to share with you how I feel about this issue.

I take the position found in my new Book of the apostle Paul where he states in:

Romans 8:29 For whom He (God) did foreknow, He also did predestinate to be conformed *to the image of his Son,* that He might be the firstborn among many brethren.

While looking into the subject of the image of the beast, I want to come out of the examination of the subject, beholding and loving Jesus Christ, more than despising the beast or his image. What do you say?

Loving our Lord and Savior is more important than despising the beast or fearing the beast whatever it does.

You students of prophecy, who haven't studied this subject for yourselves have some catching up to do. With that said, let us begin a brief overview of the books of Daniel and Revelation.

If you were to have a book of prophecy made up of only Daniel and Revelation, what you would have is a book of the history of the world from about 600 BC to the end of time.

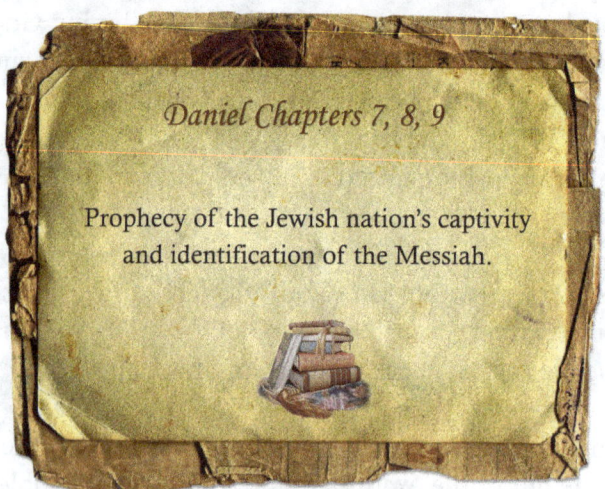

In Daniel chapters 7, 8 and 9 you have the prophecy of the Jewish nation's captivity and the identification of the Messiah.

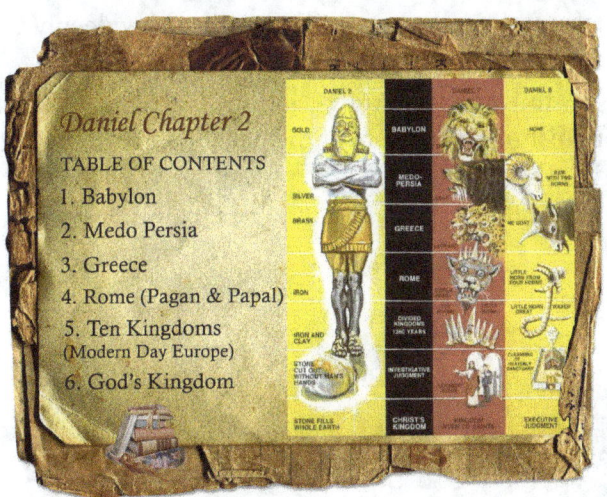

Daniel chapter 2 would contain the table of contents outlining the history of the great world empires.

Daniel 12 declares that the book of Daniel is a book written for the time of the end. By the way, Antiochus Epiphanes lived a long time before the time of the end when computer chips and bar codes could, as some believe, be used to implement the mark of the beast. So the prophecies of Daniel and Revelation are not focusing on him.

Now going from Daniel we turn to Revelation 12 that identifies a power as pagan or heathen Rome Rev. 12:4. (Recall I'm not attempting to prove these following points historically or theologically or even politically. I am only showing how deeply Christ and His Father feel about these end-time issues.)

Now in Daniel 7 and Revelation 13, you will find eight clear and distinguishing identifiers of the beast power that Martin Luther identified as the Anti Christ. This power derives its authority from pagan Rome and has the ability to implant a mark of ownership on its citizens.

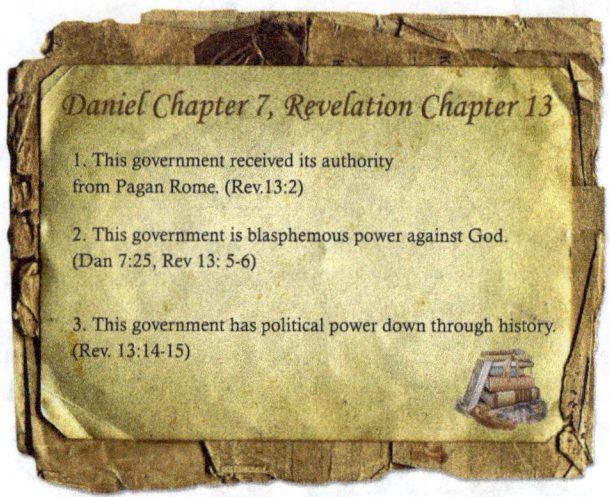

1. This government received its authority from pagan Rome.
2. This beast power and government is a blasphemous power against God.
3. This government has political power down through the history of time.

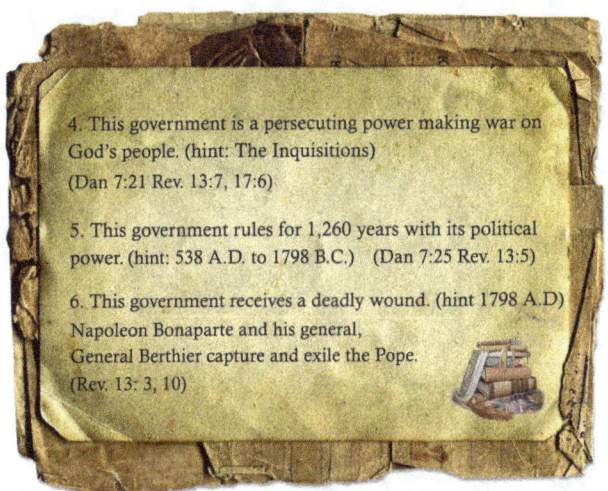

4. This government is a persecuting power making war on God's people. (hint: The Inquisitions)
5. This government rules for forty and two months or 1260 years with its political power (hint: 538 AD to 1798 AD).
6. This government receives a deadly wound (Hint: 1798 AD, Napoleon Bonaparte and the General of his army, General Berthier capturing and exiling the Pope).

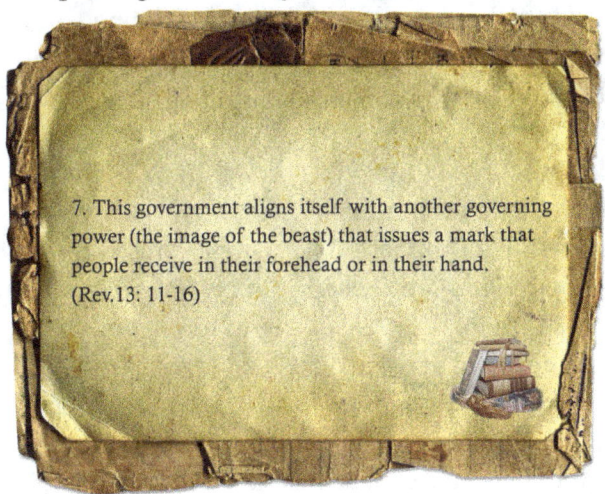

7. This government aligning itself with another governing power (the image of the beast) issues a mark which people receive in their forehead or their hand.

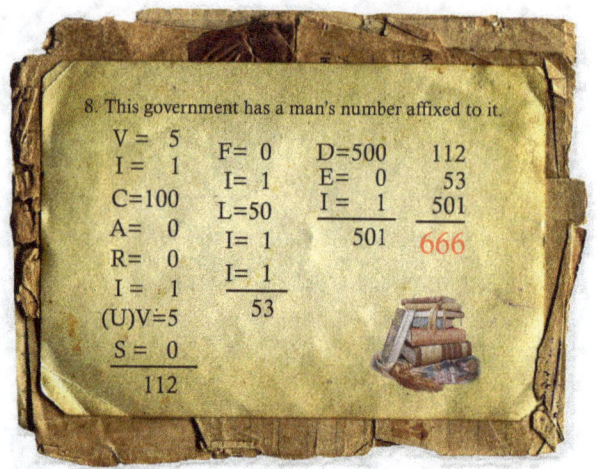

8. This government has a number affixed to it.
(Hint: Values for Roman Numerals VICARIUS FILII DEI translated Vicar of Christ, a title the Pope's of all history boast that it is uniquely theirs.)

This is the man of sin, that the great German Professor Doctor Martin Luther called the anti-Christ. The one Jesus Christ said, "Here is wisdom. Let him that hath understanding count the number of the beast, for it is the number of a man; and his number is; Six hundred threescore and six." **Revelation 13:18**

NOTE: However, this number has no significance without the other seven historical and Biblical identifiers.

So the Bible prophesied it, history verified it, and by virtue of their own admission, the religious/political power of the Vatican (the Papal institution, the beast power of Revelation 13) has dared to usurp the authority of Scripture. *It dared to transfer without scriptural authority the sacredness of the Seventh Day Sabbath to the first day of the week Sunday.*

If you doubt me, consider the following:

Quote: "It was the Catholic Church which, by the authority of Jesus Christ, has transferred this rest to the Sunday in remembrance of the resurrection of our Lord. Thus the observance of Sunday by the Protestants is an homage they pay, despite themselves, to the authority of the Catholic Church." (MGR. Segur, Plain Talk About the Protestantism of Today, p. 213)

"Question: Have you any other way of proving that the Church has the power to institute festivals of precept?"

"Answer: Had she, not such power, she could not have done that in which all modern religionists agree with her; - she could not have substituted the observance of Sunday the first day of the week, for the observance of Saturday the seventh day, a change for which there is no scriptural authority." (Stephen Keenan, A Doctrinal Catechism, p. 174)

Finally, this is from a reprint of the editorials of the Catholic Mirror by the International Religious Liberty Association published in Chicago, entitled 'Rome's Challenge: Why Do Protestants Keep Sunday?' (a quote from the Archbishop of Reggio, at the Council of Trent.)

"The Protestants claim to stand upon the written word only. They profess to hold the Scripture alone as the standard of faith. They justify their revolt by the plea that the Church has apostatized from the written word and follows tradition. Now the Protestants claim that they stand upon the written word only is not true. ***Their profession of holding the Scriptures alone as the standard of faith is false***"(emphasis mine)

Proof: The written word explicitly enjoins the observance of the seventh day as the Sabbath. They do not observe the seventh day but reject it. If they do truly hold the Scriptures alone as their standard, they would be observing the seventh day as enjoined in the Scriptures throughout. Yet they not only reject the observance of the Sabbath enjoined in the written word, but have adopted and do practice the observance of Sunday, for which they have only tradition of the Church. Consequently, the claim of 'Scripture alone as the standard' fails; and the doctrine of 'Scripture and tradition' as essential is fully established, the Protestants themselves being judges. (Again emphasis mine)

(Footnote 7 See the proceedings of the Council; Augsburg Confession; Encyclopedia Britannica, article "Trent, Council of.")

Daniel 7: 25 And he shall speak great words against the most High, and shall wear out the saints of the Most High, and *think to change times and laws*: and they shall be given into his hand until a time and times and the dividing of time. (1260 years)

II Thessalonians 2: 3,4

3 Let no man deceive you by any means: for that day shall not come, except there come a falling away first, and that man of sin be revealed, the son of perdition;

4 *Who opposeth and exalteth himself above all that is called God,* or that is worshipped; so that he as God sitteth in the temple of God, (The Vatican) shewing himself that he is God.

The Scriptures declare in regard to Satan:

Isaiah 14:12-14

12 How art thou fallen from heaven, O Lucifer, son of the morning! how art thou cut down to the ground, which didst weakens the nations!

13 For thou hast said in thine heart, I will ascend into heaven, I will exalt my throne above the stars of God: I will sit also upon the mount of the congregation, in the sides of the north:

14 I will ascend above the heights of the clouds; *I will be like the Most High.*

Only the God of the universe Himself can change the laws that govern the universe and that is the foundation of His government. As a well-known Bible teacher once said, "If I was Satan and I saw a day that was set aside to honor the Creator who made me, I would be so furious about that I would determine to something about it." Well, Satan did, through the institution of the Vatican.

At this point in my testimony, I want to take the same position as Martin Luther and pray the prayer that he wrote to his family in 1540.

> Oh, Christ my Lord, look down upon us and bring upon us thy Day of Judgement, and destroy the brood of Satan in Rome. There sits the Man, of whom the apostle Paul wrote (II Thessalonians 2:3,4) That he will oppose and exalt himself above that is God,- that Man of Sin, that, that son of Perdition. What else is papal power but sin and corruption? *It leads souls to destruction under thy name O Lord…*I hope the Day of Judgement is soon to dawn. Things can and will not become worse than they are at this time. The papal see is practicing iniquity to the heights. *He suppresses the Law of God and exalts his commandments above the commandments of God.*
> (Prophetic Faith of Our Fathers, Volume 2, page 281) (Emphasis mine)

My story and testimony are not comparable to Martin Luther, I have likened them to my journey through life. A life that began on a cold morning of November the 27th day of the year 1944 in the town of Poplar Bluff, Missouri, a young boy who was adopted into a family of that community.

As that young boy who was raised up in a lifestyle that held seeds of disastrous consequences that were sown in his young and fertile mind; that boy missed the truth hid from him in a church that was also ministering in the darkness of error. That boy against this backdrop of darkness, would throw away an opportunity to give and live his life for his Lord and Savior. A young boy who would grow into manhood and would be plunged from the heights of sinful pleasure into a twenty-three-year living nightmare because of deep spiritual deception. Much like a King named Nebuchadnezzar did so many years ago.

This young boy in becoming a man, failing in all aspects of his life, failing in relationships from living in a dysfunctional family, failing in his ability to maintain self-control, and even failing of maintaining life itself.

Yet despite all this brokenness, sorrow, and pain resulting in long years of mental illness, *the God of Love and Mercy* looked down from Heaven with compassion upon this broken life. And because of the intervention of His Son on a cruel cross two thousand years ago, intervened in this pitiful example of a life; giving him hope and assurance of salvation.

> **Psalm 51: 17** The sacrifices of God are a broken spirit: a broken and a contrite heart, O God, thou wilt not despise.

Not only did He defeat the enemy of mankind's happiness on that lonely hill that day. Nineteen hundred and ninety-three years later, He would defeat the great adversary once again and free a broken man from the oppressive power of that enemy. Two thousand years ago Christ cried, "It is finished", and on June 17, 1993, He proclaimed once again "It is finished" and He set this captive free!

Then in His great and tender love, He brought me into the glorious and wonderful experience of His New Covenant.

> **Hebrews 8:10** For this is the covenant that I will make with the house of Israel after those days, saith the Lord; *I will put my laws into their mind, and write them in their hearts: and I will be to them a God, and they shall be to me a people:*
> **Galatians 2:20** I am crucified with Christ: nevertheless, I live; yet not I, but Christ liveth in me: and the life which I now live in the flesh I live by the faith of the Son of God, who loved me and gave himself for me.

II Corinthians 5:17 Therefore if any man be in Christ, he is a new creature: *old things are passed away; behold, all things have become new.*

And the most glorious transaction in God's Universe:
II Corinthians 5:21 For He has made Him to be sin for us, who knew no sin; that we might be made the righteousness of God in Him.
Colossians 1:27 To whom God would make known what is the riches of the glory of this mystery among the Gentiles; *which is Christ in you, the hope of glory.*

This brings to a very important point I want to make. This journey from my revelation of darkness into the revelation of His marvelous light reminds me of a story about Jesus during His journey through this life. It's a story about responsibility.

While Christ, in His journey was teaching His disciples in Jerusalem His path crossed with a blind man begging alongside the road. I found this story in my *new Book* in the book of John. If you have your Book, read the complete story for yourself—it's beautiful. It reminds me so much of my story. I'm only going to share enough of it to make a point.

John 9:1-5 And as Jesus passed by, he saw a man which was blind from his birth.
2 And his disciples asked him, saying, Master, who did sin, this man, or his parents, that he was born blind?
3 Jesus answered, Neither hath this man sinned, nor his parents: *but that the works of God should be made manifest in him.*
4 I must work the works of him that sent me, while it is day: the night cometh when no man can work.
5 As long as I am in the world, I am the light of the world.

This is what I believe the Lord said to me in the story of my life. *"The purpose of your experience is not to cast blame on anyone but that the glory of God might be revealed. As long as I am in the world, I am the light of the world."*

What I have attempted to share with you in this testimony is what my new Book calls "the glory of this mystery …which is Christ in you, the hope of glory"(Colossians1:27).

It's the glory of Christ revealed by the angel of Revelation that comes down from Heaven. Having great power that lightens the earth with his glory, a glory that is given as a gift to an undeserving and sin-plagued people. That is why this heavenly gift, given so freely to sinful human beings by the heavenly ministry of Christ Jesus and the Holy Spirit, constitutes the special aspect of the everlasting gospel spoken of, in the book of Revelation.

> **Revelation 18:1** And after these things I saw another angel come down from heaven, having great power; and the earth was lightened with his glory.
> **Revelation 14:6,7** And I saw another angel fly in the midst of heaven, *having the everlasting gospel to preach unto them that dwell on the earth*, and to every nation, and kindred, and tongue, and people,
> 7 Saying with a loud voice, Fear God, and give glory to Him; for the hour of His judgment is come: and *worship Him that made heaven, and earth, and the sea, and the fountains of waters.*

Obviously then there is something about this angel's message from Heaven in respect to worshiping Christ the Creator instead of worshiping the beast which constitutes "good news". Despite that "good news" Christ Himself still feels strongly about this issue of worshipping Him and His Father instead of the beast or receiving his mark or the number of his name for He says in His Book:

> **Revelation 14:9,10** And the third angel followed them saying with a loud voice. If any man worship the beast and his image and receive his mark in his forehead or in his hand.
> 10 The same shall drink of the wine of the wrath of God, which is poured out without mixture into the cup of His indignation; and he shall be tormented with fire and brimstone in the presence of the holy angels, and in the presence of the Lamb.

You don't get much stronger feelings than that. Have mercy! But that is how strong God feels about this end time issue of worshipping the beast power instead of Him.

Thou shalt have no other gods before me…Thou shalt not bow down thyself to them, nor serve them: for **I the Lord thy God am a jealous God. Exodus 20:3,4**

However in light of Scripture and my testimony, here is what I believe and think the good news is in this message.

In my *new Book*, there is a book called Deuteronomy. In that book, there is a very special text I wish to share with you.

Deuteronomy 5:15 And remember that thou wast a servant in the land of Egypt and that the Lord thy God brought thee out by a stretched out arm: *therefore the Lord thy God commanded thee to keep the Sabbath holy.*

I like the way Today's English Bible puts it, "Remember that you were slaves in Egypt and that I the Lord your God, rescued you by My great power and strength. That's why I commanded you to observe the Sabbath."

But you may say that the text were written for the Israelites and not for us as modern-day Christians. Allow me to ask you a question. What does Egypt represent? Was not Egypt the capital city of a false worship system with it gods of the Nile, gods of the underworld, and its Pharaohs who ruled and were to be worshiped as sun gods? History is very clear at this point.

Can then ancient Egypt, the capital of a false worship system be equated with Revelations Babylon, the mother of harlots?

History again testifies to the truth that Babylon was the center of a false worship system. With Nimrod worshipped as the sun god, Tammuz, etc, and all their other gods and goddesses.

The Bible and Biblical scholars equate spiritual Babylon in the book of Revelation with a corrupt religious system of worship.

Revelation 17: 5 And upon her forehead was a name written, MYSTERY, BABYLON THE GREAT, THE MOTHER OF HARLOTS AND ABOMINATIONS OF THE EARTH

A false system of worship so corrupted it calls forth an announcement from an angel directly from heaven itself.

REVELATION 18
"After these things I saw another angel come down from heaven, having great power; and the earth was lightened with his glory. 2. And he cried mightily with a strong voice, saying, Babylon the great is fallen, is fallen, and is become **the habitation of devils**, and the hold of every foul spirit, and a cage of every unclean and hateful bird."

Therefore, I see the text of Deuteronomy 5 as applicable to us in this generation, as it did for the Jews in their generation.

For as I have shared with you in my testimony, and witness that I had become the recipient of the consequences of worshipping in a false worship system (and my own foolish choices). A worship system that has dared to, without authority from Scripture, yet boasting of their power to do so, transferred the sacredness and holiness of the Seventh Day Sabbath to a common workday of the week, Sunday. This unauthorized changing of God's Law is not only non-biblical but is an unholy sacrilege with eternal as well as secular consequences.

This ancient yet modern false worship system declares its leader as equal to God and to be revered as God.

What I wish to share with you now is an article I read about—and which has haunted me as I followed the death of Pope John Paul II and the election of Pope Benedict XVI. All the pomp, circumstances, and ritual rivaled any earthly Monarch, King, Queen, or President. As I heard one Catholic priest put it "the Vatican has owned the airwaves for the month of April", I certainly agree with him it was unprecedented.

Yet should we be surprised for the Scriptures prophesied in Revelation 13:3 "all the world wondered after the beast."

The following is a quote from that article. The article is called "Prompta Bibliotheca". Translated from Lucius Ferraris, the article titled "Papa", Volume VI, and pages 26 to 29.

"The pope is of so great dignity and so exalted that he is not a mere man, but as it were God, and the vicar of God.... The pope is of such lofty and supreme dignity that, properly speaking, he has not been established any rank of dignity, but rather has been placed upon the very summit of all ranks of dignities. ...The pope is called most holy because he is rightfully presumed to be such....The pope alone is deservedly called by the name 'most holy' because he alone is the vicar of Christ, who is the foundation and source and fullness of all holiness... 'He is likewise the divine monarch and supreme emperor, and the king of kings'...Hence the pope is crowned with a triple crown, as king of heaven and of earth and the lower regions...

Moreover, the superiority and the power of the Roman Pontiff by no means pertain only to heavenly things, to earthly things, and things under the earth, but are even over angels than whom he is greater...So that if it were possible that the angels might err in the faith, or might think contrary to the faith, they could be judged and excommunicated by the pope...For he is of so great dignity and power that he forms one and the same tribunal with Christ..."

The article goes on to state,

"The pope is as it were God on earth, sole sovereign of faithful of Christ, chief of kings, having plenitude of power, to whom has been entrusted by the omnipotent God direction not only of the earthly but also of the heavenly kingdom… *The pope is of so great authority and power that he can modify, explain, or interpret even divine laws.*" (emphasis mine)

The arrogant claims of the religious/political system almost leave one breathless but it was prophesied that it would happen, in the Word of God. (Daniel 7:25)

Therefore with the biblical and historical evidence before us, that has been documented and demonstrated and arrogantly proclaimed by the papal institution itself; *I see the Sunday worship system as a confrontational attack upon the authority of God and His Almighty Sovereignty and constitutes, as evidenced, being the mark of the beast.*

Any religion or false worship system that wars against the Sovereignty of Almighty God robs His people of the power and the glory that is found in Jesus Christ alone.

Daniel 7:25 And he shall speak great words against the most High and shall wear out the saints of the Most High, *and to think to change times and laws.*

He thinks to change law and time sacred to the Christ Jesus the Creator of heaven and earth; a law and time that the Sovereign of the Universe has placed in the center of His Ten Commandment Law that governs heaven and earth.

A sacred moment of time placed in His law that has come under attack and controversy. Mankind stands at the head of a false religious *system that has removed that sacred moment of time called the Seventh Day Sabbath and replaced it with another moment of time the first day of the week called Sunday.*

The leader of this religious system demands that those who subject themselves to that system of worship show their loyalty and obedience to that change by keeping the first day of the week sacred instead of the Seventh Day Sabbath.

No one or object in heaven or earth is the being that can demand obedience, for the God of the Law of Ten Commandments is the one who created all things. Only Jesus Christ the great Lawgiver and the one who perfectly represented that Law to the world could make such a change in that sacredness of that day or that Law. And nowhere in Holy Scripture is it recorded that He did or attempted to make such a change.

The Fourth Commandment Law is a weapon that can be brought against false worship. For this Law cannot be applied to any false god, rulers, or false religious systems to command worship on a false man-made Sabbath. Mankind who "has not made heaven and earth, the sea, and all that in them is" has no such biblical authority."

For in six days the Lord made heaven and earth, the sea, and all that in them is, and rested the seventh day: wherefore the Lord blessed the Sabbath day, and hallowed it.

The pope and the Vatican make a lot of claims such as the power to absolve sin, the power to create the Creator through the doctrine of transubstantiation, the ability to stand as the mediator between God and man, and the list goes on. *But one thing he cannot lay claim to, is being the Creator of heaven and earth, the sea, and all that in them is.*

The author of this Law has declared who He is, the extent of His dominion, and His right to rule that dominion.

Therefore every created being must acknowledge that Christ Jesus and He alone who is the Creator of all things has the exclusive right to demand obedience from all His creatures, including Catholics, Popes, Cardinals, Bishops, Priests, Parishioners, Protestant Clergy,

Protestant Ministers and Protestant Church Members, Jews, Muslims, Hindu, Atheist, etc.

This Law written with God's own finger has His signature and contains the Seal of His government and authority. This Law is forever binding upon his true people who in loving loyalty, happily subrogate themselves to His Law of Love and Liberty.

The pope claims that he has the right to be called most holy because he is rightfully presumed to be such....

Even Christ, whom the pope claims being his vicar, said of Himself:

> **Matthew 19:17**.....Why callest thou me good? there is none good but one, that is God: but if thou wilt enters into life, keep the commandments.
> **Matthew 23: 8-10**
> **8** But be not ye called Rabbi: for one is your Master, even Christ; and all ye are brethren.
> **9** And call no man your father upon the earth: for one is your Father, which is in heaven.
> **10** Neither be ye called masters: for one is your Master, even Christ.
> **II Thessalonians 2:3,4**
> **3** Let no man deceive you by any means: for that day shall not come, except there come a falling away first, and *that man of sin be revealed, the son of perdition;*
> **4** Who opposeth and exalteth himself above all that is called God, or that is worshipped; so that he as God sitteth in the temple of God, (the Vatican) *shewing himself that he is God.*

The article entitled "Papa" stated also that the pope alone is deservedly called by the name 'most holy' because he alone is the Vicar of Christ, who is the foundation and source and fullness of all holiness...'He is likewise the divine monarch and supreme emperor, and king of kings'...

King of Kings is a sacred title reserved for only one and that one is *Jesus Christ the Lord.*

Revelation 19:11-16
11 And I saw heaven opened, and behold a white horse, and He that sat upon him was called Faithful and True, and in righteousness, He doth judge and make war.
12 His eyes were as a flame of fire, and He had a name written, that no man knew, but He Himself.
13 And he was clothed with a vesture dipped in blood: and His name is called the Word of God.
14 And the armies which were in heaven followed Him upon white horses, clothed in fine linen, white and clean.
15 And *out of His mouth goeth a sharp sword, with it He should smite the nations; and He shall rule them with a rod of iron: and He treadeth the winepress of the fierceness and wrath of Almighty God.*
16 And He hath on His vesture and on His thigh a name is written, KING OF KINGS, AND LORD OF LORDS.

Even the religious leaders and teachers of Christ's day understood that no man is a mediator between God and sinful man to usurp the power of God to forgive man of his/her sins.

Mark 2:7 Why doth this man thus speak blasphemies? who can forgive sins but God only?
I Timothy 2:5 For there is one God, and one mediator between God and men, the man Christ Jesus.

We, as Christians, are justified by faith in Christ and our sins are forgiven by the sacrificial offering of Christ's shed blood as the penalty for our transgression of the Holy and Sacred Law of God. Not by acts of penance, receiving the Eucharist, the saying of rosaries, prayers to dead saints, or trips to the Holy See.

Being made right with God, what is called *justification*, is again through faith in Jesus Christ and the reception of the righteousness of Christ by faith that will be manifested in obedience to all the commandments of God.

Ephesians 2: 8 For by grace are you saved through faith and not of yourselves; it is a gift of God.
Rev. 14:12 Here is the patienceof the saints: here are they that keep the commandments of God, and the faith of Jesus.

However, because of this false worship system's influence upon God's people, many have lost sight of Jesus as the only mediator between God and mankind. No man, not even a pope or Protestant minister can usurp Christ as our only hope of forgiveness and salvation.

Satan knows that one of the greatest deceptions is that it is of no consequence what we believe as God's people; *for he knows that the love of the truth and the reception of it sanctifies the believer and prepares them for translation.*

Paul speaks of those who receive not the love of the truth whereby they might be saved. Because of this, God shall send them a strong delusion that they maybe lose their salvation who believe not the truth, but have pleasure in unrighteousness.

Paul speaks of those who receive not the love of the truth whereby they might be saved. Because of this, God shall send them a strong delusion that they maybe lose their salvation who believe not the truth, but have pleasure in unrighteousness.

II Thessalonians 2: 3-14

3 Let no man deceive you by any means: for that day shall not come, except there come a falling away first, and that man of sin be revealed, the son of perdition;

4 Who opposeth and exalteth himself above all that is called God, or that is worshipped; so that he as God sitteth in the temple of God, shewing himself that he is God.

5 Remember ye not, that, when I was yet with you, I told you these things?

6 And now ye know what withholdeth that he might be revealed in his time.

7 For the mystery of iniquity doth already work: only he who now letteth will let, until he be taken out of the way.

8 And then shall that Wicked be revealed, whom the Lord shall consume with the spirit of his mouth, and shall destroy with the brightness of his coming:
9 *Even him, whose coming is after the working of Satan with all power and signs and lying wonders,*
10 *And with all deceivableness of unrighteousness in them that perish; because they received not the love of the truth, that they might be saved.*
11 *And for this cause God shall send them strong delusion, that they should believe a lie:*
12 *That they all might be damned who believed not the truth, but had pleasure in unrighteousness.*
13 But we are bound to give thanks always to God for you, brethren beloved of the Lord because God hath from the beginning chosen you to salvation through sanctification of the Spirit and belief of the truth:
14 *Whereunto he called you by our gospel, to the obtaining of the glory of our Lord Jesus Christ.*

All power is given into Christ's hand that He may dispense rich gifts to His people, imparting the priceless gift of His righteousness to those of us who see ourselves as helpless, sinful, and sin-damaged human beings, unable to attain Christ's righteousness, power, and glory, in and of ourselves. I don't know about you, but to me, *that is good news, and that's what the gospel means!*

These rich gifts are freely given to us as believers by Christ, is a source of wonder and awe. This gift, Christ's righteousness sent to us from Heaven is the gift that brings all other gifts in its train. The gift that brings victory from defeat, joy over sadness, life instead of death. It's the *gift of Christ in you* the hope of glory!

And once again, any religion or false worship system that wars against the Sovereignty of God rob God's people of that glory which is found in Christ alone.

Yet, God, Himself has promised that the glory of Christ will be restored in His people.

The Lord Jesus Christ's prayer expresses and promises it.

John 17: 9,10
9 I pray for them: I pray not for the world, but for them which thou hast given me; for they are Thine.
10 And all Mine are Thine, and Thine are Mine; and I am glorified in them.

Revelation 3:11,13
11 Behold I come quickly: hold that fast which thou hast, that no man take thy crown.
13 He that hath an ear, let him hear what the Spirit saith unto the churches.

In His love for people, He has given us a warning. He is not going to allowing sin and a sin-cursed world with its false religious system to go on forever. He is going to bring it to a sure finish and give us a brand new start and brand new world with the government upon His shoulders. The Bible calls it the New Earth.

Isaiah 65:21-25
21 And they shall build houses, and inhabit them; and they shall plant vineyards, and eat the fruit of them.
22 They shall not build, and another inhabit; they shall not plant, and another eat: for as the days of a tree are the days of my people, and mine elect shall long enjoy the work of their hands.
23 They shall not labour in vain, nor bring forth for trouble; for they are the seed of the blessed of the Lord, and their offspring with them.
24 And it shall come to pass, that before they call, I will answer; and while they are yet speaking, I will hear.
25 The wolf and the lamb shall feed together, and the lion shall eat straw like the bullock: and dust shall be the serpent's meat. They shall not hurt nor destroy in all my holy mountain, saith the Lord.

Isaiah 66:22,23
22 For as the new heavens and the new earth, which I will make, shall remain before me, saith the Lord, so shall your seed and your name remain.
23 And it shall come to pass, that from one new moon to another, *and from one Sabbath to another,* shall all flesh come to worship before me, saith the Lord.

The Lord in His Word also teaches that this Old World with its corrupted religious systems is going down. *For the Lord, Himself will take it down with a whirlwind of devastation the Bible calls the seven last plagues (Rev. 16). But before He does He in His great love for us lets us know so we won't go down and suffer with it.*

Revelation 18:8 Therefore shall her plagues come in one day, death, and mourning, and famine; and she shall be utterly burned with fire: *for strong is the Lord God who judgeth her.*

There are many true and loving Catholics, Protestants, and Bible-believing Christians without denominations, or even those perhaps worshipping in heathen religious systems, yet our Heavenly Father loves them all and has tender regard and sympathy for their spiritual blindness that to a large measure they are not responsible for. I think of the beautiful Mother Theresa. Who can find fault in such a loving, kind, and saintly woman? And also the wonderful hospital founded by Danny Thomas. How many children have been blessed by the founding of Saint Jude's hospital?

My contention is not with God's beautiful children in any denomination but with the Vatican's counterfeit religious system, with its corrupt hierarchy. Not the wonderful, sincere people in the Catholic Church, or the sincere but deceived Protestants, or any of God's people wherever they worship.

God loves all His people very tenderly, so He calls His people out of this fallen system of worship.

I want to make another thing very clear. *No one has received the mark of the beast, who is attending a Sunday keeping worship church or thinking they are keeping Sunday sacred, by worshiping on that day.* No one will receive the mark of the beast until the day comes that worshiping on Sunday is mandated by the legislative power of the United States Congress which will then *constitute a merging of church and state which is the image of the beast.*

The reason the Scriptures names the Vatican the beast power is because she has always been copulation of church and state, that history has shown to persecute God's people.

Revelation 14: 8,9,10
8 And there followed another angel saying, Babylon, is fallen, that great city, because she has made all nations drink of the wine of the wrath of her fornication.
9 And the third angel followed them saying with a loud voice. *If any man worships the beast and his image*, and receive his mark in his forehead or his hand.
10 The same shall drink of the *wine of the wrath of God*, which is poured out without mixture into the cup of His indignation and he shall be tormented with fire and brimstone in the presence of the holy angels, and in the presence of the Lamb.
Revelation 18:4 And I heard another voice from heaven, saying, Come out of her, my people, that ye be not partakers of her sins, and *that ye receive not of her plagues.*

Come out - but to where? As I shared with you earlier, I am not a member of any denomination or church organization, not Catholic, Protestant, Evangelical, Charismatic, etc. I just love the Lord, His people, and His Word. So I am not beating the drum, if you will, for any church organization.

I have been called by the Lord and was given a mandate, with the gospel commission, as many others, to warn His special ones who love Him, with Christ's warning message of love, that a cruel deception has been perpetrated on them by the enemy of their eternal welfare.

This counterfeit religious system is designed to make His people forget Him while all the while thinking that they remember Him.

And as shared earlier, to rob God of the power and glory that belongs to Him and His people, given to them by our Lord Jesus Christ.

This deceptive counterfeit worship system is going to be destroyed before Christ's second coming and our Heavenly Father and His beautiful Son does not want His children to be destroyed with it. So, He has given to me, along with many others this mandate so as to warn his children so as not to lose their eternal inheritance.

So again, I ask, come out to where?

Come out from falsehood to the truth, from error to enlightenment, from darkness to the light, from the false worship religious system to Scriptures' true worship system, from Sunday worship to Sabbath worship.

You can worship the Lord of the Sabbath in your home, with a group of Seventh Day Sabbath keepers. You can find a group of people that meet on Sabbath in their homes or other places of gathering. Or you can find a Sabbath-keeping church if you desire so. My point is that this is between you and the Lord. No person can dictate how or where you are to worship the King of Kings.

Despite the deceptions and our blindness, we are still called God's people—*wondrous love and divine compassionate Savior.*

Scriptures teach that the warnings that Christ gives to us the whole world will wonder and be in awe of this false religious worship system with all its mesmerizing pomp and circumstance, processional grandeur, boasts of miracle-working power through it deceased saints, and of course its worldwide political power and influence.

Revelation 13:3,8
3….And all the world wondered after the beast.
8 And all that dwell upon the earth shall worship him, whose names are not written in the book of life of the Lamb slain from the foundation of the world.
The Lord Jesus Christ has emphatically warned us not to be taken in by such things.

Matthew 24:24,25 *For there shall arise false Christs, and false prophets, and shall shew great signs and wonders; insomuch that, if it were possible, they shall deceive the very elect.*
25 *Behold, I have told you before.*
Matthew 25:13 *Watch, therefore,* for ye know neither the day nor the hour wherein the Son of man cometh.

Having our confidence in a false worship system and in men who have changed Heaven's Law for man's laws places us in harm's way and is a very dangerous undertaking.

I will dare to say that if our nation had remained true to the Scriptures, that the terrible tragedy of September 11, 2001, would never had happened. For Scripture also teaches that as long as God's people stayed true to His covenant He protected and delivered them from their enemies. It is through His Law and covenant that He protects His people.

Psalm 91:4 He shall cover thee with his feathers, and under his wings shalt thou trust: *his truth shall be thy shield and buckler.*
Psalm 119:145-151
145 I cried with my whole heart; hear me, O Lord: I will keep thy statutes.
146 I cried unto thee; save me, and I shall keep thy testimonies.
147 I prevented the dawning of the morning and cried: I hoped in thy word.
148 Mine eyes prevent the night watches, that I might meditate in thy word.
149 Hear my voice according unto thy lovingkindness: O Lord, quicken me according to thy judgment.
150 They draw nigh that follow after mischief: they are far from thy law.
151 Thou art near, O Lord; and *all thy commandments are truth.*
(Including the fourth)

Because of you *Oh Lord and your protective love and care* I shall not be afraid, I pray in Jesus name.

Psalm 91:5-7
5 Thou shalt not be afraid for the terror by night; nor for the arrow that flieth by day;(nor for airplanes that flieth by day)
6 Nor for the pestilence that walketh in darkness; (terrorism, biological warfare, Covid- 19, or chemical attacks, nuclear attacks or dirty bombs) nor for the destruction that wasteth at noonday.
7 A thousand shall fall at thy side, and ten thousand at thy right hand; *but it shall not come nigh thee.*

Therefore because of His protective love and care, that He made possible by Christ lovingly shedding His shed blood and because of the great love Christ has shown, I can't bear the thought of ever being separated from Him. I choose to love and follow Him of whom the Scriptures speak. How about you?

Acts 3:22,23
22 For Moses truly said unto the fathers, A prophet (Christ Jesus) shall the Lord your God raise up unto you of your brethren, like unto me; *Him shall ye hear in all things whatsoever He shall say unto you.*
23 And it shall come to pass, that every soul, which will not hear that Prophet, shall be destroyed from among the people.

I have attempted to answer the question posed in the very first paragraph of this book I have written. "Why doesn't God act sooner on behalf of those suffering mental illness, mental disorders, and anyone else that find themselves in situations that they don't understand or are too difficult for them to overcome by themselves?"

I would sum it up this way. It is not God's fault. He has poured out all heaven in that one gift of Jesus Christ, who came to set the captive free. Cast your helpless soul upon Jesus Christ and believe that He will help you. Trust Him for He is trustworthy. Like the little song goes – "Trust and obey for there's no other way to be happy in Jesus, only trust and obey."

I have biblically and historically attempted to show that it is because mankind with its false religious systems has robbed God's Word of its power by warring against His Majestic Sovereignty; causing those who are placing their trust in their religious leaders, in a false and counterfeit religious system, to have their follower's best interest at heart. When in reality they are deceiving, misleading, and robbing them of the glory and power of God's Word freely given to them in Christ Jesus.

Because of that, many of us fall victim to Satan's power that only finds satisfaction in inflicting pain and suffering on humanity in the form of mental illness, senseless deaths, murders, child abusers, sex offenders, etc. In short, every tragic event reported on the twenty-four-hour cable news networks.

Many of us have unwittingly have given ourselves into the hand of our enemy (Satan), and have given him the absolute right to oppress and afflict us. This is why the translation preparation by keeping God's commandments by the indwelling Christ and by His power is not an option. It is vital and constitutes a part of the everlasting gospel.

Revelation 14:6-7

6 And I saw another angel fly in the midst of heaven, having the everlasting gospel to preach unto them that dwell on the earth, and to every nation, and kindred and tongue and people. 7 Saying with a loud voice, Fear God, and give glory to Him; for the hour of His judgment is come: and worship Him that made heaven and earth, and the sea, and the fountains of waters.
Therefore:

- I am determined by God's grace and love to have the seal of God placed in my forehead and His Father's name written upon my heart.
- I am determined by God's grace to be like John Bunyan's Christian pilgrim when asked at the gates of the Celestial City for his certificate, will be able to show it to the angelic gatekeeper. Sealed with the seal of God with Christ's Father's name and the New Jerusalem written on my heart.
- I am determined by God's grace to keep Christ's holy Law and

Commandments that He has written upon the tables of my heart in the New Covenant experience including the fourth, enjoining me to honor His Seventh Day Sabbath.
- I am determined by God's grace to obtain a translation preparation to honor Jesus Christ at the Marriage Supper of the Lamb.
- By God's grace I am determined to heed the message of the three angels.
- *By God's grace I am determined not to align myself with a false worship system that wars against the Sovereignty of Almighty God.*
- I am by grace determined to be one of those voices crying in the wilderness, "The kingdom of Heaven is at hand, make straight the way of the Lord, make a highway for our God."
- By God's grace I am determined to confront the counterfeit religion of the Vatican, and apostate Protestants Leaders that keep God's people in bondage with false doctrines that challenge the Lord's Sovereignty.
- I am determined by grace to issue Christ's challenge to those Church leaders keeping God's children bound to this earth with its sins, suffering, and sorrow, with their counterfeit and false religious system, that wars against the Sovereignty of Heaven's God and government "Thus saith the Lord, to His people "Come unto Me that you receive not of her plagues.
- I am determined by the sovereign grace of Almighty God to the writing and publishing of this book, and to testify that by faith in vision I saw a coming of an angel down from Heaven. He was clothed with heavenly power. He comes to the earth. Only those spiritually dead, yes even those twice dead and plucked up by the roots would fail to recognize his presence. Light flashes everywhere. Dark places are lighted up. He utters his voice in thunderous tones.

Babylon the great is fallen,
is fallen and is become
The Habitation of Devils.

And they overcame him by the blood of the lamb, and the word of their testimony; and they loved not their lives unto the death.
Revelation 12:11

ACKNOWLEDGEMENT & REVIEW

A Personal Appreciation

I want to extend a personal and warm heartfelt thank you to all the members and staff of the AEGA team of which, without their professionalism and skilled knowledge, my testimony in the form of this book would not have been possible. May our Lord send showers of blessings and much success upon AEGA Design Publishing Ltd.

The Pacific Book Review

The Habitation of Devils: Why God Doesn't Act reads like a memoir. Author Dan R. Overfield writes about his life, his family history, the ups and downs of life, overcoming challenges, learning as well as unlearning, being a believer; all by recounting how he tries to live righteously. I enjoyed reading Dan R. Overfield as an author because of how authentic his style of writing is. Paging this book, one realizes the author does not force anything, as the entire content in his book flows naturally. The reader feels as if they are part of the author's journey and his experiences.

The Habitation of Devils: Why God Doesn't Act is appropriate to a wide reading audience, and particularly is a book every reader who is in any form of despair should read. The author assures one of God's love, discusses living with imperfections and waiting for the right time. This book will get readers to be more spiritual, and learn more about God and themselves as being a child of God.

www.ingramcontent.com/pod-product-compliance
Lightning Source LLC
Chambersburg PA
CBHW070053120526
44588CB00033B/1419